THE CONFERENCE

A SHORT NOVEL

WILEY YINGER

WILD YOOT BOOKS

Yinger, Wiley.

The Conference / by Wiley Yinger
ISBN 0991375726

1.   Mystery—Humor—Fiction. I. Title

ISBN 978-0991375721

For

Ryan

DAVENPORT

It was Friday morning and Giles Davenport was in front of the bathroom mirror brushing his teeth thinking about tomorrow night. He wasn't paying attention to it, but his reflection was that of a handsome man of some forty-five years with a full head of brown, grey-free hair and keen blue eyes. His looks probably put him in the running for the job that he's held for the past twenty years, as he was often in front of cameras, but it was his intellect and speaking skills that sealed the deal. Giles Davenport was the Minister of Information for the Office of Justice, and it was his job to brief the media on all subjects related to the Office. He had excelled in the position because he could evade questions from the most dogged of reporters, but honestly Giles had to give his wife Linda most of the credit. She was the smartest person he had ever met, and being with her just made him better at his job. It didn't hurt that she was in the PR game as well. If he could duck some of Linda's questions, no reporter had a chance.

Tomorrow was their twenty-fifth anniversary, and for the past several months Linda had been hinting at trying something "new" in the bedroom, and Davenport had been doing his best to try to elude, evade, and plain dodge the subject as it came up from time to time. It wasn't that he was particularly sheepish or a prude, he just wasn't sure it was a road he wanted to go down. He turned his head and looked at the bed to find one of Linda's legs poking out of the duvet. Her sleepy eyes noticed him and she smiled. He knew there was this vague sort of countdown, and by the look she just gave him he knew she was going to bring it up within a matter of seconds, so he quickly spat out the toothpaste in an attempt to change the subject before it even came up. Being this close to the "deadline" he also knew it probably wasn't going to work.

"How long has it been since we went up to see Jr. and Ellie?"

"About the same time we last talked about it."

Davenport looked at himself in the mirror and shook his head. "It's not that I don't want to talk about it, it just never seems like the right time." Davenport scrunched up his nose and pulled out an offending hair. "I swear Linda every year I get hairier. Places I never would have dreamed possible."

"It's really not that bad Giles, it just takes a little more time to groom. It happens to all of us. We're all just pretending we're not animals."

"I suppose you're right," Davenport said as he straightened his tie. Linda passed by him, turned on the shower and got in.

"You never wait," he said.

"What?"

"You never wait till the water gets warm before you get in."

"I always take a shower after you. The water's already warm."

"Huh."

"Giles it doesn't mean anything if we do it. It's not going to define you. Did you confirm our reservations for tomorrow night?"

"Yup, we're all set," Davenport said as he rolled his eyes at his reflection and walked out of the bathroom.

"How's it going with Clog?"

"About the same, this week he's been running around the office pissed off at some guy named Burt. He's a jackass." Davenport sat down on the bed and put on his shoes.

"Screw the public sector Giles, when are you going to come around and work with me."

"You've been trying this for years Lind. You're already the boss here. You want to be my boss twenty-four hours a day?"

"You know it wouldn't be like that Giles, you'd be a partner," Linda said, her voice echoing in the shower.

"It's your firm Lind. Besides, we both need our space. We'd get sick of each other pretty quickly."

"We've been married for twenty-five years Giles."

"Together for twenty-eight I know. Your point?"

"You'll always be my Duckie."

"Jesus Christ." A smile crept to lips as he stood up and put on his suit coat. He heard a text message alert from his phone and walked over to it. "Crap it's Ziempa," he said as he slid the phone in his pocket, "I gotta head out early girl."

"Why?"

"Something big at the office. Clog wants me there as soon as possible."

"Ice cream and waffles Davy!"

"I'll make it for us tomorrow Lind."

"Okay see you later. Think about it."

"I will."

"Not that."

Davenport shook his head as he made his way to the front door. He grabbed his keys and he was out. In the elevator he was thinking about the *Pretty in Pink* reference. He hadn't heard it for a while. Everything that woman does is on purpose. Everything. Goddamn eighties, thought Davenport.

Now Giles was in a time machine when Linda was the drop dead and he was still five feet eight. She saw it though. Even way back then she saw it and that was that. They had been together ever since. Davenport grew five inches that summer and put on twenty pounds and the acne vanished. They screwed like rabbits for three straight years. She can still make his stomach go goofy every once in a while. Yup he got his dream girl. As the elevator doors opened he concluded he was a lucky bastard.

CLOG

Milton Clog circled an acronym at the top of a legal pad several times and felt effervescent. He had just finished leading the office's Friday morning aerobics class that he himself invented. He called it "Fast Forward Fridays," where the group would choose a workout DVD and put it on 1x fast forward. Milt was really the only one who could keep up with the frantic, jerky movements and most of the class just stood around and watched. There was usually one person that tried to give it a go, and this Friday it was Dutch Rodriguez. Dutch found out it brought the burn pretty fast, and the idea of shedding a couple pounds for his daughter's upcoming quinceañera wound up pulling a groin for him and sending him limping out of the session early. There were always casualties from the battle of the bulge, thought Milton. But this morning had just been a warmup for the upcoming trial. Milt looked at his watch and it was about to begin. Never would he have thought that peanut butter could bring him such hardship and such providence in less than twenty-four hours. Now he was going to be able to be free, free to spend his days as he desired. He put the pen down, raised himself out of his chair and immediately started doing jumping jacks. Today is the day, he thought, today will make other dreams feel bad about themselves.

After thirty-odd years as the Director of the Office of Justice, Milton felt he owed it to himself to live a little. Milton was an avid at-home ultra-marathoner, a relatively new sporting phenomena and it showed, literally to the bone. Milt was a tall man, but that physical endowment was hindered by his extreme lack of muscle and flesh. Although standing around six feet five inches, Milton barely weighed one hundred sixty pounds. This was all due to his extreme workout regimen, and the fact that he rarely chewed and swallowed anything. The mental picture would be complete if one could imagine a giant condom vacuformed onto a skeleton.

The reason why Milton never participated in "real" ultramarathons was because like many Americans from the United States, he felt that wherever he was was his, which really meant he only felt comfortable where he had always been. Online ultras became the perfect outlet for his cultural agoraphobia and social introversion. All he needed to feel good about himself was the fitness tracker on his wrist, his phone, the internet, and his bag of bones. The anonymity made him interminably satisfied, so much so that his handle for the competitions became *ultraman351*, but poor Milt really didn't piece together that there were three hundred fifty other dipshits out there just like him.

In his mind he was also a world traveler. He'd been all

across the globe in online ultras, where participants downloaded their cardio data onto a leaderboard, and he had actually done quite well in the "Arctic Assdragger" and the "South American Sweater," each race well over one hundred miles. But recently the Director was looking for something more, and last month it was announced the first annual "Everest Open" would commence. It was a race from Lukla airport to the top of the great peak, traversing up and down through its many villages along the way. At a mere twenty-four miles it wasn't even a regular marathon, but the Open had something much more challenging in store for those daring enough to try. Unlike previous virtual ultras, altitude would be a major factor in results, meaning that the higher one was on the race route, the ratio of heartrate and steps taken to distance traveled would shrink. There were also acclimatizing points and simulated weather delays where no advances were allowed, so the participants would have to exercise at the whim of the organizers. This was no small hurtle to success.

The historic event was predicted to take somewhere between five and seven days, and last Saturday morning the contestants were virtually dropped off at the Tanzing-Hillary airport in Lukla, Nepal from a simulated flight from Kathmandu. It was then a race of some nine hours to the elevation of 3,400 meters (11,280 feet) where the village of Namche Bazaar is located. The contestants were then to acclimatize for a day, and much to Milton's chagrin encouraged to browse online Nepalese gift shops for baubles and gewgaws to support the local economy and raise funds for the Village Development Committee. The Director was on the fence about it until he read the fine print and found out that each purchase of ten dollars or more would afford the consumer a ten-minute deduction from his or her time. Milton parted ways with $39.98 plus shipping in the acquisition of a 3"x 5" Tibetan mouse rug and a 6" Nepalese desk prayer wheel. Milton closed his eyes after he clicked confirm and imagined himself in the death zone. Those twenty minutes could be the difference between living and dying.

And so it went. Higher and higher the entrants climbed, Monday was Namche Bazaar to Tengbouche, Tuesday Tengbouche to Dingbouche where, at 4,410 meters (14,468.5 feet) it was time to acclimatize yet again. Milton was rather glad he had Wednesday to himself, and for a fleeting moment he thought in retrospect he should have taken a few personal days instead of taking on the daunting task within the parameters of his office. Yesterday he had taken the steps up to the thirty-seventh floor, and to his dismay found that he had only advanced a mere 75 meters (246 feet). He was completely incredulous by his lack of distance and emailed a complaint to the organizers whom had yet to respond. Needless to say the altitude had become quite a thorn in his side, yet Milt was still determined to brave the conditions, especially after he checked the leaderboard and found that *ultraman300*, who, after Milt checked his profile, was a native Arizonan in a wheelchair laid up with a newly installed titanium hip and competing in the "virtual-surrogate" category, was ahead of him some 1,600 meters (5,249 feet) by way of placing his fitness tracker on a hind leg of his Jack Russell named Burt. The man had even posted a video of the little bastard running around the yard chasing a drone. The damn thing was so fast it was a blur. It was then Milt's belly caught fire, and he spent most of Wednesday afternoon walking in place while trying to figure out the perfect combination of calisthenics that would propel him past that charlatan *ultraman300* and on toward Gorak Shep.

Thursday was the day of reckoning. The grueling leg from Dingbouche to Gorak Shep would prove, Milt hoped, *ultraman300's* comeuppance. The Director took a deep breath, squirted two packs of energy gel into his mouth and began his predetermined routine. It was an eclectic mix of upper and lower body calisthenics—Dive Bombers, Beach Scissors, Good Mornings, Dirty Dogs, One-Legged Romanian Dead Lifts, Beat Your Boots, The Arabesque, and finally to top it all off Ham Sandwiches. After an hour and forty-five minutes Milt scrambled to his desk, flopped down in the chair exhausted and waited for his data to upload to the website. The Director suddenly stood up in horror and looked more closely at his phone to make sure what he had initially seen was true. "Goddammit!" Milt screamed, for the bastard *300* was still ahead of him by 500 meters (1,600 feet). It was now time to get serious, enough was enough, so Milt fired four more packets of gel and began, with renewed strength to catch that goddamn dog.

By the afternoon he was sprawled out on the floor and more than once had to shoo away his worried assistant Marie so he could focus his mind for tomorrow. What was the use? He was still way behind Burt and he resigned himself to the conclusion that all was lost. Demoralized, dejected Milt lay on the floor of his office and began to weep. It was imperceptible at first, he merely looked like he was going to sneeze, but slowly the sorrow and self-pity began to convulse his whole body with every beat of his broken heart. He wailed softly to a god that no longer existed, to a life that held no more meaning when he heard the tell-tale Tibetan chime ring out softly from his pocket. It meant an update from the race, and Milt cleared his eyes with his shirt cuffs and pulled out his phone. He sniffled as he began to read and slowly, proudly his sense of manhood began to return. He began reading faster and faster, the words blazing across his mind. "Burt …" "Drone out of charge …" "Crash …" "Propeller guard compromised …" "On our way to vet." Milt sat up with a start. He couldn't believe what he was reading! *Ultraman300* was in the back yard of his house putting Burt through his paces when the drone ran out of charge and crash-landed. Being that Burt had never caught the contraption before he went bonkers when he finally did and tore the thing apart, apparently swallowing a piece of plastic in the process. After an hour or so Burt was visibly impaired, and *ultraman300* pieced the drone back together and found a part of the propeller guard missing. He immediately figured what was wrong and took Burt directly to hospital.

Fortune was smiling down at Milton, and he was not going to let it go to waste. He started to his feet, grabbed his suit coat and made his way to the door. He whizzed past Marie, telling her he'd see her in the morning and made a mad dash for the stairwell. He felt a lightness in his feet, a renewed vim that propelled him down the thirty-seven floors as if it were a dream. All he could think about was putting a virtual beat-down on the infirmed terrier. He hit the pavement and began fast-walking around the block. Again and again the familiar sights beckoned him for another revolution, another soothing, non-threatening lap around the same four corners. After the thirteenth or fourteenth loop he noticed the hot dog vendor outside his building waving his arms and gesturing to him with a bottle of water. The Director welcomed the idea and grabbed the bottle with a wink, and on the subsequent lap gave the vendor a five-dollar bill, and received a quarter back after he rounded the block yet again. The universe was aligning for Milt and Milt alone. He felt it in the bones that were so close to his skin. His hips were charging forth to the rhythm of his pumping arms. It was as if his wing-tipped shoes were treading on clouds. Could he? Would he dare? Yes! He was going to walk the six blocks to his apartment. He was going to do it this time! Milton confidently broke away from his orbit and started to head home. He pulled out his phone to check his distance from Burt and as soon as he unlocked it the Tibetan chime, once a ring of hope and promise now tolled unmercifully as it brought Milt's worst fears to bear. A video post from *ultraman300* showed Burt galloping on a treadmill. The camera panned in on the console and he was running at 12 mph! The caption read: "All clear! Vet gave Burt bread and peanut butter and he's doing fine! See you all at base camp!" Milt screeched to a halt and looked up to the firmament. "Motherfucker!" wailed the Director as he stood on what seemed to be a deserted street corner. He lowered his head in defeat and hailed a cab.

        A profound shroud of melancholy wrapped itself around Milton on the two-minute ride home. He paid the driver and walked somberly up the stairs to his apartment. He felt like the apex of the mountain as he opened the door—alone and cold, attainable only for the briefest of moments if at all, languishing among the myriad ranges but alone just the same as it peeked up through the troposphere almost into the stratosphere. He took solace from his position at the Office of Justice as he was in rarified air to be sure. He concluded he too was the mountain.

The Director slumped wearily into his Barcalounger and tried to hum a dirge befitting the mournful occasion. His close-mouthed voice cracked at times with sentiment, swelled at times with hope, and finally turned soft and tired with a genuine humility and a resignation that in this end everything would soon be all right. There were other ultras to be had, other races to be run. If he remembered correctly the "Dubai Dropper" was in three-weeks' time. Yes he would be ready, he would put this unfortunate event behind him and rise to the next occasion. It was at that moment when Milton was beginning to drift into a sleep the indomitable chime, that siren of the Himalayas came calling once again. Milt half-heartedly reached into his pocket and squinted at the screen. Weather . . . Weather Delay! The Director couldn't believe it. What luck! What pleasure oh what grace! He feverishly checked the leaderboard as a bit of his tongue poked through his lips. A dead heat! He and Burt had apparently pushed past the checkpoint at Gorak Shep and traversed its sand covered lake to base camp! Incredible! Milton's phone shook in his hand as he read the weather report. The station at South Col reported heavy winds in excess of 150 km/h (93mi/h) and the organizers could not in good conscience let anyone up the mountain. The race would continue at 8:30 a.m. EST Friday. Milton sighed as he clicked his phone off and through his exhaustion and excitement shortly passed out. Thus went Thursday night into such dreams as daring as victory.

The Director finished his two hundred-fiftieth jumping jack when he heard a knock on his door. He said come in and a short, pudgy man with three or four days of stubble tentatively walked into the room. The look on his face said to Milton that he may be looking for some advice as to how to properly tuck in his shirt.

"What are you doing here so early Ziempa? And tuck in your shirt for god's sake we're professionals here!" He watched Ziempa fumble around his waist and jab his open hand down his pants at various points as he spoke.

"You called me an hour ago sir, said to come in immediately. I have the latest on the Dabney case."

"That's right that's right," the Director said as he reached for his towel and dried himself off. He pulled out his phone and nodded approvingly. "Damned if I'll be bested by some fifteen-pound shit eater."

"Sir?"

"Nothing, nothing Ziempa. Are McMusker and Quinlap on the scene yet?"

"Yes sir, they just got there."

"Good. Let me know when Davenport gets in, I'm going to want to talk to him about what we're going to do about the conference for this mess. And make sure you send him a copy of what we have so far. After you do that head down to the hotel. I want to know what the hell is going on down there."

"Yes sir."

"How many patrolmen in the ER?"

"Thirty-five sir."

"A goddamn mess Ziempa!"

"Yes sir." Ziempa watched the Director look back down to his phone and stood waiting for an irrefutable sign that the conversation was terminated. After several moments of silence Ziempa decided to take initiative. "Sir do ..."

"That's all Ziempa for Christ's sake! Can't you see I'm busy here! Let me know when Davenport gets in."

"Yes sir," said Ziempa as he accidentally backed into the closed door and startled himself, turned around and opened the door and walked out.

"The door Ziempa!"

"Yes sir."

The door closed and the Director looked down to his phone once more. He began to walk in place and think about what he was going to say to Davenport, but more pressing was the cooldown/warmup in preparation for the impending and treacherous Khumbu Icefall that lay ahead. He indeed had his work cut out for him.

IT BEGINS . . .

Davenport shook his head in disbelief as he click-closed the file. He rubbed his forehead with the palm of his hand then slid it down his face until it covered his mouth. I'm screwed blew through his fingers as he thought about that chubbo Ziempa in his office ten minutes before and that dense look on his face when he gave him the news.

"Did you hear?" Ziempa said, standing sheepishly before the threshold of Davenport's office, his pudgy face filled with concern that he may have to be the one to do it.

"What?" Davenport replied, knowing he was going to have to say it again.

"You mean you haven't heard?" Ziempa took a few steps toward Davenport's desk.

"Ziempa why is it that you ..." Davenport didn't care enough to continue so he just said what again. Ziempa looked up stupidly from the open he was fiddling with. "We just got a file from McMusker, you better open it up. The Director's coming to see you in twenty minutes." Ziempa turned around and began walking out of the office but not before saying the name "Dabney, Cleland B." Davenport watched him stop and then start walking again like he wasn't quite sure where to go. "Boob," Davenport said to himself as he typed the name into the database.

That was ten minutes ago. Two minutes ago, Davenport had to close the file for the sheer complexity of its potential explanation, but the Director was coming to see him in eight minutes, so he opened it back up. A range of emotions washed over Davenport's face as he reread the file of Cleland Bainbridge Dabney and the circumstances that brought him to his attention. There was shock, dismissal, and concern, followed by shock and bewilderment, followed by shock and surprise, followed by fear, and finally … dread. He knew why the Director was coming to his office. It was going to be him. Every damn time it was him. Explaining the demise of twisted Jacks. He sighed I'm screwed.

It wasn't just because of the circumstances that surrounded Mr. Dabney's expiration that he felt so screwable— apparently the man had done nothing illegal, just really really weird. As Davenport scoured the file it became more and more apparent that the initial assumption that any layperson would make would be generated by their own particular illicit tastes. Cleland Dabney may have been a little south of level but he was no criminal. Everything was explainable, thought Davenport. All the animals were one thing. Even the clothes had a potential explanation, but the peanut butter? Jesus Christ. Peanut butter— those two words can bring out the worst in people, and he was quite sure the worst was going to muster in that damn conference room.

He spent the next several minutes with his hands over his face, thinking about what could've happened and what he could do to get out of it when he heard a perfunctory knock on the free side of his desk and looked up to see the Director. His stern face showed little concern for the fact that he was not the one to have to do this or that Davenport was.

"Davenport," he said, "Davenport I assume you ..." the Director stopped for a moment when he saw Davenport's chin fall to his chest, then continued. "Good. This is big Giles. Do you know who C.B. Dabney is?" The Director waited. Davenport looked up. The Director pushed his knuckles off the desk and stood up straight. "You don't. Not too many people do. He's the only heir to the Dabney Plus-Size Baby Clothes Corporation. He's worth billions. He had no wife Davenport, no husband, no girlfriends, no boyfriends, no children, no relatives, no lovers of any ..." The Director suddenly paused, not wanting to jump to the conclusion he had already made. "The only things he leaves behind is his will. And all those animals."

"What does that ..."

"Everything Giles," the Director said with certainty. He threw his hands behind his back and began pacing back and forth in front of the desk. Milton wanted Davenport to think this expression extemporaneous, but in all fairness he had practiced the speech earlier this morning during his daily walking in place session. He suddenly came to a standstill. "A criminal act needs no explanation," the Director insisted. "We as justice officers merely state the facts, and it's the job, no the right, the duty

Davenport, of every citizen to make up their own mind. We are the deliverers of truth, and sometimes the truth hurts." The Director lowered his head in reverence for his own words. Davenport gambled on how long the moment of silence was going to take.

"Listen Milt ..."

"His name must not be cleared!" The Director threw up a quivering index finger, almost stunning himself by his lack of control. Davenport stood up from behind his desk. "I've gone over the file and it seems ..."

"Popular opinion Davenport. That's what we've got on our hands now. What am I telling you for?" The Director asked the question like he really did want an answer. "Well?"

Davenport shrugged.

"The day's been tits up since dawn," the Director admitted. "The uniforms on the scene couldn't keep this to themselves and spilled it all over the wires. I've been informed coffee's been firing out of nostrils all up and down the precincts since this morning. Hell some of them couldn't even keep hold of their blasted cups at all!" The Director's face looked mystified by their lack of discipline as his eyes glued to some grim, eventual horizon. "Couldn't even hold their FUCKING CUPS! Jesus H. Christ Davenport we've got ten patrolmen in the ER with first degree sinus burns and twenty-five with singed testicles and labia!"

"Listen Milt ..."

The Director's face twitched slightly as his index finger pointed repeatedly to the window. His voice suddenly became low and deliberate. "The press has been outside Dabney's hotel since 6 a.m. and now there's a vigil gathering on the corner in prayer for the animals and a rally for the induction of members into the newly formed Damnation for Dabney Association." The Director now changed arms and began pointing fervently in the other direction. "On the other side of the street an assemblage of revelers has gathered, presumably in exaltation of Dabney's questionable character." The Director paused in an attempt to intensify the gravity. "There have been several unconfirmed reports of indiscriminate fondling." Suddenly in the Director's pants began a kazoo rendition of *Hail to the Chief.*

"Milt there's no evidence here to …" The Director thrust one hand up to pause the conversation and the other into his pocket for his phone. He saw on the screen Ziempa's fat, unshorn face.

"It's Ziempa," he whispered and covered the camera with his thumb. "What is it Ziempa!"

"The downtown sir …I can't see you sir …"

Ziempa's eyes blinked vacantly as he searched around his blank screen.

"Yeah there's something wrong with the … What is it Ziempa!" The two men watched Ziempa suddenly blush for a moment as they heard people in the background catcalling his ample caboose. It was only a few moments before his eyes began to smolder with relish.

"For Christ's sake get down to business Ziempa!"

"The downtown sir, there are lots of tents set up down here," wiggled Ziempa's face in the Director's hand, "and lots of …"

"Hold on Ziempa!" The Director thrust a hand on top of

the receiver and began to whisper. "Davenport you have to get down there. Give the press something on the way in. Check the scene and come back here for the debrief."

"This is horse shit."

"That's live TV down there Davenport. You know how fickle it can be."

"Get Ziempa to do it."

"Get Ziem ... Now listen goddammit! The Director quickly collected himself by looking down at his tie and smoothing it out with his hand. He looked up gravely. "Peanut butter's involved Davenport. There's little choice. We gotta give 'em what they want."

10:01

Davenport reluctantly acquiesced to the Director's demands as he drove up to the scene. As an officer waved him through the barricade he looked around at all the commotion. It was typical of something of this magnitude, just the signage different. "Down with Dabney" signs hopped up and down with impunity on one side of the street, while on the other, peanut shells in the shape of a jubilant set of dick and balls waved from side to side like depraved metronomes counting mixed meter. He had been here a hundred times before—the blinding lights, the fake shutter snaps, the clouds of coffee breath, yet as Davenport stopped the car in front of the high-rise, with the reporters surrounding the vehicle something seemed different. He sat there for a few moments, imagining himself trying to answer ridiculous questions when an overwhelming urge to flee welled in his mind. He imagined himself at the conference, trying to explain the situation, all the while inextricably linked to Cleland Dabney and his barnyard escapades. A lesser man would have wept. Davenport merely sighed and opened the door to the cacophony of chants, megaphones buzzing gibberish, and reporters' harebrained questions. He threw his hands up as he got out of the car as if he were pushing on the air around him, gesticulating hold on a fucking minute. The crowd of reporters like an amoeba swallowed Davenport and moved anomalously around him, shifting and transforming as Davenport, now its nucleus, walked to the awning of the building. Upon reaching the entrance, a patrolman lifted the caution tape and Davenport stooped under it like a prizefighter and walked up to the edge of the police line. He then stood with the stern countenance of a schoolmarm as he waited for the throng of eager journalists to settle down and stop blurting out ridiculous questions. He looked around when he heard the most juvenile of them and sure enough—Billings and Raybach. Those two idiots' minds were always playing hopscotch in the gutter.

In the moments before the crowd became quiet Davenport realized the reasons for which he was given this position so long ago and why, after all these years he had retained it. A sense of himself inexplicably appeared, as if the occasion alone, like a reaction from the lips to hot soup, or the mind's unkempt conclusions when seeing the smallest crack of any ass was enough to jolt him back into being. In his mind he began to smile, for after all these years, in all these meetings with the press, he had never felt more like himself, never more willing to send absolutely no information to anyone. He realized again his canvas and his muse, and that he was the best. He began with a sentiment and tone that could only be confused with moral.

"While in fact we have neither the answers nor the motives behind this unfortunate situation as of yet, I would ask all cooperation be afforded the Office of Justice as it swiftly ascertains the facts that surround Mr. Dabney's lapse into the unknown, and for our part, as concerned and dedicated professionals, is to take the appropriate time to pause until those facts become manifest. Within the hours that follow, we enjoin not only the media, but the populous to make truth a matter of record, only employing what has been proven, leaving behind what we would merely admire to contrive."

Silence.

The crowd began to rumble, back and forth their faces with the same look like *what the hell was that? Did he just ...* They began to gather an opinion as their voices concluded they needed to start asking some questions but before they could, Davenport suddenly looked as if he were deep in thought, giving the impression of some sort of internal struggle, even hesitating at times to speak, as if any second he could cave and admit some damning piece of evidence.

When he was sure he had their attention Davenport breathed deeply, turned around and walked into the hotel. The amoeba looked pissed. Stuck behind the police line the reporters resorted to raising their microphones in the air and shouting against the charade as they watched the glass turnstile cease revolving. They may as well have been holding torches.

Davenport's smile shrank back into his mind as he made eye contact with the concierge. He was about to show her his badge when she recognized him.

"Good morning Mr. Davenport. The express elevator to the penthouse is demarcated by Mr. Buelfarbel, the hotel manager." Davenport nodded and followed the direction of the concierge's open arm. The man in front of him was probably in his fifties and in good shape, with the adornments on his coat and hat Davenport thought he looked like a cross between Denzel Washington in *Flight* and Idris Elba in *Pacific Rim*.

"Mr. Buelfarbel," Davenport said and extended a hand.

"Mr. Davenport," Buelfarbel said and shook it. They got on immediately splendidly. Buelfarbel opened the elevator and they both entered. As the doors closed Buelfarbel pressed the button to the penthouse. He began to smile as Davenport sniffed.

"You'd think it would smell a little, wouldn't you Buelfarbel?"

"They didn't come up this way. There's a freight elevator around the corner. You want to take that one?"

"We'll take it on the way down."

"Okay."

"So what do you know Buelfarbel," Davenport asked as he threw his hands in his pockets.

"I got a call from the night manager around three-thirty this morning telling me there had been a noise complaint about the penthouse, and being that it was C.B.'s place and she knew about the animals she asked me what to do."

"What did you tell her?"

"I told her don't do anything and I'd be right there. By the time I got up to the penthouse it was about four-thirty. I spent the next half hour knocking on the door. When there was no response I called Mr. Fuss."

"Mr. Fuss?"

"Kilroy Fuss. He's the superintendent of the Dabney farm. I explained what was happening and he told me something must be wrong and to call the police. He told me not to enter the penthouse without them, so I waited for the patrolmen to get here and we went in."

"How long have the animals been up there," asked Davenport.

"I would say we had them all up there around eight yesterday morning, so a little over twenty-four hours," said Buelfarbel.

"None of your business?"

"None of my business. I was just doing my job. Of course there was the various ordinances regarding livestock in the hotel, but we looked the other way."

"Why was that?"

"Well it's his hotel."

"Of course."

"All I heard was that C.B. was really excited to have them here ... and something about a photo shoot. I make it a point not to listen too much."

"Can you give me Kilroy's number?"

"Sure," Buelfarbel said as he pulled out his phone, found the number and showed it to Davenport.

"Thanks."

"We're almost there."

"Good. Mr. Fuss ... Giles Davenport from the Office of Justice. Oh you are? Very well. I look forward to meeting you too sir. Yes a tragedy indeed ... Goodbye." Davenport returned the phone to his pocket and looked over to Buelfarbel. "He's on his way. Said he be here posthaste."

"Posthaste. Very considerate men both," Buelfarbel said as he opened his arm to the elevator doors that were beginning to separate. "This is the anteroom and officer Monfries, who seems to look a wee peaked."

"Hey Buelfarbel. Good morning sir," said Monfries as she took off her hat.

"You know you've made a lot of people relatively un-comfortable today Monfries," Davenport said as he made sure to look her up and down. "Next time keep your lips around your teeth."

"Yes sir."

"Fine. Now what the hell is this?" The three looked down to another patrolman who was seated on the floor rocking his back against the wall. After a few tense moments Monfries confessed.

"This is Meltzman, first through the door. He's been like that since it happened," Monfries said as she bent over and waved a hand in front of Meltzman's face. "I guess he's still trying to work it out." Monfries stood back up. "We got a call from the hotel around five this morning because of a noise complaint about the penthouse. I was behind him. He took the brunt sir."

Davenport bent over and gave Meltzman a healthy smack to the cheek. "Meltzman!" Davenport waited and watched as the officer's eyes rolled around in his head for a few seconds. "Snap out of it son," Davenport said as he threw his hand out and pulled the boy to his feet. "What did you see

Meltzman?"

"I … I …" Meltman's eyes darted frantically around the room.

"I'll give you another one Meltz …"

"I opened the door. They … they were all together, dressed up like they were at a wedding. In in in a circle. Licking each other." Meltzman put a shaky hand to his brow.

"Go on son," Davenport said gingerly.

"They all stopped doing what they were doing for a few seconds to look at me, to stare at me. Then they all just started doing it again, like I wasn't even there. Like I had seen nothing. Dabney's naked body lying in the middle of them sir."

"All right Meltzman. All right." Davenport patted the patrolman on the shoulder.

"Monfries?"

"He just started backing up till he hit the wall. Wound up how you saw him. I went in and checked for vitals but nothing. Came back here and called it in. I don't think he noticed the trapeze. Probably would have made things worse."

"I agree. Mr. Buelfarbel, would you please escort officer Meltzman to the lobby and bring Mr. Fuss up when he arrives?"

"Of course," Buelfarbel said as he helped the officer enter the elevator, all the while whispering words of encouragement.

"Oh Buelfarbel?"

"Yeah."

"Those detectives inside, did they talk to you?"

"Wanted nothing to do with me." The elevator doors began to close as Buelfarbel gave a wry smile. Davenport turned to Monfries.

"I saw McMusker's name on the file. He still inside?"

"Yeah McMusker and Quinlap," Monfries said as she stood looking at the ground. Davenport decided to give her a verbal pat on the bum.

"You'll know for next time Monfries."

"Yes sir."

"Go get something to eat. Let me know when Beck gets back with Fuss."

"Yes sir," Monfries said.

"The freight elevator Monfries."

"Yes sir."

THE SCENE

Davenport watched Monfries walk dejectedly around the corner when he felt and heard his phone ringing. He pulled it out of his pocket and his chin fell to his chest before he answered. "Hey Lind ... no I haven't ... I can't give you an answer right now I'm at the scene and I ... You're where? ... Jesus Chr ... Linda sweetheart can we ... Linda we said we were going to talk about ... okay ... okay ... I haven't agreed to ... all right ... all right I'll see you later ... bye ... yup bye." Davenport rolled his eyes and shook his head as he slid the phone back into his pocket. Now I gotta deal with fucking McMusker, Davenport said to himself as he stood in the anteroom. He gave himself a few moments to gird up his loins, and in so doing noticed emanating from the door a faint aroma of cow shit. "Okay," he said as he opened the door and poked his head through the doorway.

"You boys decent, or do you need more time?"

"What?" said McMusker, not bothering to turn his rotund body around as he stood shooing away a goat that was playfully nosing one of his giant ass cheeks. "What's with these fucking goa ..." he finally jerked around with a start and nudged the beast away with a foot. It walked away bleating as if offended.

Davenport opened the door and saw and smelled and heard the totality of the situation. The smells obvious for sure, the cows offering the most excrement to the penthouse's odor, but as he looked around his discerning olfactory sense and the gentle wafts from various tails brought a significantly broader picture to mind. Indeed the regular barnyard droppings were present, but there was something else ... Davenport suddenly realized he could no longer dally with inefficiencies and quickly snapped himself out of it. "How many and what species Dan," asked Davenport as he cocked his head to a border collie that stood in front of him barking. The dog seemed emphatic, yet the barking sounded like a succession of hoarse farts.

"Is that a saddle?"

"What?" McMusker said as he threw a hand around his ear and tried to lean above the din of cows mooing, a rooster crowing, pigs oinking, chickens clucking, ducks quacking, a horse whinnying, and goats bleating. One of the goats ran up to Davenport and immediately fell into spasm and onto its back. Its legs quivered as they pointed up to the ceiling before gently falling to the floor as the goat rolled onto its side. Davenport rightly stepped aside to give the animal its proper berth. The dog began sniffing the goat's hooves.

"They've been doing that all morning!" McMusker bellowed, "I knew you'd be down Davenport! Fucking weirdest scene ever, it even beats …"

"I don't want to hear it, much less talk about it!"

"Fair enough, but I told you one day …"

"What?"

"What?"

Davenport gave a fake nod like McMusker just did, keeping the fuck you strictly between themselves. "Where's Quinlap?"

"What?"

"Quinlap," Davenport said as he watched his step and moved a little closer.

"Bathroom. Some kinda monkey came outta nowhere and stole the glasses right off his face. You know Quinlap, he took it personally and started chasing the damn thing around the place. Couldn't tell ya how many times he fell down. Little shit still has 'em too … look." McMusker pointed to the other side of the room. "Little bastard's taunting us." The monkey looked like it was laughing as it hopped up and down trying unsuccessfully to don the spectacles. Davenport turned, and then McMusker— Quinlap exited a bathroom, steam and all some fifty feet away with a white towel wrapped around his waist. The two men watched him as he moved his clothes from the washer to the dryer. Davenport regretted being able to see him whistling.

He nodded to McMusker and they made their way around the animals to the other side of the room. A chicken tripped up McMusker for a second. They climbed over the doggy-gate into the hallway and found Quinlap back in the bathroom.

"You're doing laundry at a scene Quinlap," Davenport asked.

"What else do you want me to do Dan, there's crap everywhere, and that fucking mon ..." Quinlap turned from looking at himself in the mirror to Davenport. "Shit."

Davenport turned to McMusker. "That little gate kept them all in?"

"Most of 'em could've either flown, jumped, or just busted it down."

"But they didn't."

"Nope."

"You add anything to the file since nine?"

"A fewwww things," McMusker groaned as he traversed the blockade again. "I think we've pieced together the wedding party. The bride and groom are the pigs over there, we could tell, the ah groom has the cummerbund with rhinestones, so we figured they're an item. Let's see here ... ." McMusker grabbed the pen from his shirt pocket and threw it between his lips and it disappeared underneath his enormous mustache. He reached into his back pocket with his other hand, pulled out his notepad and flipped it to a blank page. The pen seemingly fell out of his facial hair into his hand. "Yeah there's not much taffeta left, but the cows were the only ones other than the pig wearing any so, you know, bridesmaids." He cleared his throat and pointed the pen across his chest to the horse. "He's a groomsman, along with the rooster. They both have the same bow tie as the pig. We figured the rest just attendees."

"Finished?" Davenport said as he raised an eyebrow.

"Yup."

"You find any of his clothes?"

"Not a stitch. You think he was wearing clothes?" McMusker cracked a smile.

"Why didn't you talk to Buelfarbel?"

"Who's Buelfarbel?"

"The hotel manager."

"I thought he was a bellhop."

"Jesus Christ." Davenport shook his head and looked around the room.

"What the guy looks like a general from the salvation army."

"He takes his job seriously Dan."

"Yeah well the epaulets are a little much."

"Fair enough. What else?"

"Davenport the guy fell off a trapeze naked and broke his neck. Crime scene was here for like ten minutes and then the paramedics left... what?" McMusker began following Davenport around the perimeter of the room when Davenport suddenly stopped in front of one of the windows. "The lemur threw this," Davenport said as he pointed to a big glob of peanut butter on the curtain.

"The monkey? You're reading too much into this one just like ..." McMusker stopped short when Davenport turned around.

"Don't you and Quinlap have other cases?"

"Yup."

"Then see if he's finished primping and get the hell out of

here."

Both men turned to a knocking on the door. Monfries stepped into the room cautiously, half way through a hotdog. "Buelfarbel's outside with Fuss," she chewed. "Do you want me to ..." her eyes suddenly grew wide as she saw the monkey making a beeline for her and quickly pulled the door closed in defense of her sandwich.

"I'll go get Quinlap," McMusker said and began lumbering to the bathroom. That one goat followed him. Davenport walked over to the door and opened it to find Buelfarbel and Mr. Kilroy Fuss. The two men introduced themselves in person and shook hands.

"A firm grip and please, call me Kilroy." There was a gleam in the old man's eyes that bespoke a youthful energy and vitality Davenport had rarely seen in other septuagenarians. He wasn't quite sure about Kilroy's accent, but he figured he was originally from somewhere in the UK or Ireland. Maybe coming to the states when he was a boy made him lose what was once a definable brogue.

As soon as Kilroy walked through the threshold of the penthouse all the beasts began to wander toward him. It was obvious he had a soothing effect on the creatures, and they also seemed quite relieved by his presence. The monkey noticed him first but was playing coy by running behind one of the drapes. The dog ran up to him and fart-barked a little, then ran away to scare the shit out of one of the goats so he could smell its hooves. The two huge white pigs snorted happily, thinking they were going to get some food. The cows mooed and walked a little closer. The horse clapped a hoof on the parquet floor The ducks waddled over and the chickens clucked. Kilroy gave them all a little attention before the three began touring the room.

"So it's a working farm Kilroy," asked Davenport.

"Now it is, but it didn't start out that way. Initially C.B. was just interested in raising swine for competition. These are his prized Chester Whites," Kilroy said as he pointed to the two oinkers. "They've won competitions all over the country in the past year. The gilt is named Flora and the boar Flavio. That's why they're all here. C.B. was giving them a reception before they were to mate. All the other animals were acquired by various unfortunate situations. Take Gamble for example," Kilroy called the dog over and patted him on the head. "Worst cordectomy I've ever heard. The owners were obvious imbeciles, for they left the poor canine at the farm with his tags dangling from his collar one Saturday morning. I was having my morning tea in the farm office when I heard a strange sound indeed. I couldn't quite name this sound gentleman, but I must say it did remind me of a serious bout of flatulence I once had in Barundi back in '74. As I paid more attention, the sound was too explosive and repetitious to be flatus, so I arose from my chair and went to investigate. Outside I found the collie, who is brilliant by the by, inside the farm fence herding the chickens and ducks into the henhouse. Once I got him out and found the tags I went to the home of the owners to drop him off thinking they would be relieved by the return of their beloved pet. Not so gentlemen." Kilroy looked disappointed with remembering but soldiered on.

"It was explained to me by the exasperated owners that they had done everything they possibly could to try to get

Gamble to cease his barking, finally opting for surgery. They went on to explain that in these difficult times it was necessary to find an inexpensive solution to their problem, so they had the surgery done by a first year student at the local College of Veterinary Medicine. Needless to say it wasn't a success. When the owners brought Gamble back home their three children couldn't contain themselves because of the sound he produced whilst barking. Soon the whole family ceased to take the dog seriously and produced in him a sort of melancholy. He stopped eating and drinking all together, so the owners made the decision to drop him off here. He's been right as rain ever since."

"I'm assuming the saddle is for the monkey," said Davenport.

"It is indeed. We found a few months ago Burgle had taken to riding Gamble bareback, but C.B. noticed one day that all the tugging on Gamble's coat caused him some discomfort, and as we obviously didn't have any horse tack suitable C.B. took Gamble to a local saddlery and had him outfitted. Burgle's quite the horseman, well dogsman I should say. We set up a small steeplechase in the pasture with lawn chairs and 2x4s. They both seem to enjoy it." As the men continued walking, Buelfarbel noticed the two cows' underparts. "Good lord Davenport, look at the size of those utters!"

Davenport looked down and did a double take. "Kilroy?"

"Bessie and Bessie, identical twin Holsteins suffering from *puerperal macromastia*. It's a medical condition by which the mammary glands grow abnormally large. They arrived from a dairy a few miles away from the farm. By the time they were around two and had their first calves they had outgrown the teat cups used for extracting milk. The farmers couldn't justify the expense of having extra-large teat cups specially made by an outfit in Germany, so they gave them to us, poor gals."

"I see. And the goats," Davenport asked.

"Ah yes the goats. Myotonic, otherwise known as Tennessee meat goats or Tennessee fainting goats. A hereditary genetic disorder called *myotonia congenita* causes a sort of paralysis when they feel panic ... oh there we are." The three men watched one goat faint on cue as Gamble resumed his regular place sniffing at the hooves. Kilroy had his hands clasped behind his back and walked gracefully aside the spasmodic buck as if he were in the middle of a Sunday afternoon stroll. Davenport and Buelfarbel followed closely behind.

"So how did Dabney acquire the goats," asked Buelfarbel.

"This is the strangest story I'm afraid, but quite interesting," said Kilroy as he stopped walking and turned around. "It all began with a well-meaning young lady named Myra Sternbloom. Poor Myra's parents both died a few years ago, and having no need to work because of a large endowment bestowed upon her by her parents, bought a farm neighboring C.B.'s in the hopes of turning it into a shelter for abandoned and unwanted animals. At first it was a tremendous success—in the first few months she had acquired a three legged dog, a two legged potbelly pig and an albino chinchilla. She would often come over to the farm with various husbandry questions, and C.B. and I were more than happy to accommodate her. In the next few months her shelter grew and grew. Ornery rabbits, obese felines, foul-mouthed macaws, she took on all comers which unfortunately led to her demise," Kilroy said as he lowered his head. Buelfarbel and Davenport were riveted. They both said go on.

"Of course gentlemen. Myra received a call one day from a man out-of-state inquiring if she would be interested in sheltering four goats. She said yes of course and they were shipped immediately. This is where it gets rather strange." Kilroy brought a hand to his face and began gently tapping his chin with his index finger. "Shortly after Myra took possession of the goats we received a curious phone call. C.B. and I were in the farm office discussing the latest issue of *Hogman's Quarterly* when I picked up the phone. It was Myra herself, in quite an agitated state. I put the office phone on speaker and Myra went on to explain that she was having 'spells' as she put it. Apparently whenever she was outside, for some inexplicable reason she would inevitably lose consciousness and wake up on the ground having no idea how she got there. C.B. and I came up with several impromptu diagnoses for the syncope— dehydration, diabetes, arrhythmia, anemia, but she assured us that she had been to see the doctor and received a clean bill of health. She then asked us if we would come over and witness an event. Of course we obliged and went over that very afternoon. When C.B. and I got there we found her outside mending one of her many pens. As we were getting out of the truck it happened. Myra must have hit her finger with the hammer and let out a loud 'Ouch!' that startled one of the goats and sent it into a spasm. Well as soon as she saw the goat she began to spasm as well. It was only a few seconds before they were both on the ground. In the meantime, the other goats had wandered over and as soon as Myra regained her senses and picked herself up off the ground, in her exasperation she screamed 'What the hell is going on!' which started the process all over again. So round and round it went with the fainting—goat, Myra, goat, goat, goat, Myra. Up down up down up down. It was positively hypnotic. C.B. and I were mesmerized by this strange turn of events, so we naturally let it go on for far too long. It must have been five or six cycles before we got our wits about us and started to action. We tried to round up the goats with traditional herding tactics but were met with little success. We then resorted to violent, profane outbursts with equally obscene gestures and that did the trick. We were finally able to pick up the convulsive goats and take them to the barn. By the time we returned Myra was back on her feet and as confused as ever. After our explanations and more than one incredulous look she agreed to see C.B.'s GP. She was then referred to a renowned neurologist. The diagnosis was *echopraxia capra*. It seems Myra was a sympathetic spasmodic."

"But isn't echopraxia the imitation of movements made by another person," Buelfarbel asked.

"Hence the capra," said Davenport, "so she was only responsive to goats?"

"Apparently hers was the first known case of an automatic imitation of a goat by a human," said Kilroy.

"So there are other cases," asked Davenport.

"Just yawning. It can occur across species."

"My dog makes me yawn all the time," said Buelfarbel.

"Yeah it can go both ways," Davenport said.

"When you get down to it yawning's not all that dissimilar from The Jumping Frenchmen of Maine disorder, accepting the mode of suggestion of course." Kilroy turned around, clasped his hands behind his back and began walking again. Davenport and Buelfarbel looked at each other briefly.

"The Jumping Frenchmen of Maine," asked Davenport, and he and Buelfarbel anxiously caught up to Kilroy.

"A disorder first described by neurologist George Miller Beard in 1878. Would you like me to …"

"Yes."

"Of course."

"In the remote regions of northern Maine, near Moosehead Lake there lived a community of lumberjacks that were suffering a strange affliction. Beard went to investigate this strange phenomena, and he was profoundly affected by what was found. It seems these lumberjacks had startle and tic-like behaviors, but unlike other disorders the behaviors exhibited were provoked. When given a sudden command, whether it was to jump or yell, or even hit, these men would obey the command without prejudice. There's a story, and I can't tell you it's a fact because I don't have the inclination to search for or investigate his field notes, but apparently on his first day with the men, there were six or seven present, he was standing with them in a circle and giving them various commands, like 'Slap yourself on the fanny!' or 'Call your mother a nasty piece of business!' and they were responding quite nicely to his commands. It was said that he wasn't quite sure at the time whether it was actually a disorder until the next command, whereupon he concluded it was in fact a valid malady. Against his better judgement but steadfast in his conviction to find the truth he squinted and screamed, 'Strike yourself in the nethers!' upon which he heard several groans and looked around to find all of the men on the ground in the fetal position rocking gently in extreme discomfort. The mind gentlemen, is a powerful thing." Kilroy gave no one in particular a contemplative nod.

"You mentioned the demise of Myra," said Davenport.

"You also referred to her in the past tense," said Buelfarbel.

"Horrible, just horrible," said Kilroy. "Myra was determined to 'beat' her affliction and continued to look after the goats against the continual advice from her doctors. She thought that now that she knew what was causing her ailment she could do something about it, and do something about it she did. Myra modified an old set of blinkers she found in the barn to fit her head, and began wearing them whenever she was outside. Only being able to see what was directly in front of her made it easier to keep the goats out of her sight when she was working. It also kept distractions to a minimum, so she found herself getting much more work done. She was overjoyed. Of course there was an episode every once in a while, it was simply unavoidable, and she took each one in stride. After a few months she became so used to the blinkers that she must have forgotten she had them on when she went to retrieve the mail one Tuesday afternoon. I believe it was a long haul semis coming in from Cheyenne. No charges were filed. Truly awful." Kilroy lowered his head for a moment, then raised it with the confidence of an eternal optimist. "But with every ending there's a beginning gentlemen,

and from that fateful day C.B. accepted Myra's mantle. It contin-
ues to this day," Kilroy said with a smile as he came upon the
horse. He opened his arm toward the magnificent beast.

"This is Worker, one of the finest draft horses to ever
compete. He's a Shire, all black save the white legs up to his
knees and hocks. He was put out to stud about a year and a half
ago but was unfortunately unable to perform his necessary
duties. The owners went so far as to consult an equine
psychologist and ultimately found the reason for Worker's
inopportune condition. It seems that as soon as Worker retired
from competition, he lost a sense of purpose as it were. More
precisely he had lost his ability to discern victory, being out of
the arena with no applause and no echoes from the emcee."
Kilroy turned to Worker, reached up and gently patted his head.
The giant horse shook his neck slowly and nickered
approvingly.

Davenport saw out of the corner of his eye McMusker
and Quinlap making their way to the front of the penthouse.
Kilroy turned back around to the men. "Finally the owners
decided to put Worker on a regimen of Exhausterall, you know
the ..."

"Did someone say Exhausterall? That reminds me of a
case ..." McMusker said as he walked by and snickered under
his breath.

"Just get Quinlap in the car and turn the heat up,"
Davenport said as quickly as he could, watching as Quinlap
walked bow-legged to the door to keep the chaffing from his
damp slacks to a minimum. "I'm sorry Kilroy, you were
saying?"

"Yes indeed. Worker was put on a regimen of Exhaust-erall, the male libido enhancer, and for a time was improving, but a month's supply for a human man was going to Worker every couple days, so the owners did the arithmetic and here he is. After we had Worker for a couple days C.B. had a PA system put into the paddock and when Worker came in from pasture we'd play the last thirty seconds from Pink Floyd's *Fearless* on a loop and take turns giving him various distinctions over the loudspeaker. It wasn't exactly the same, but you could tell as soon as Worker heard those claps and chants his gait would stiffen and his head would bob up and down in sweet remembrance." Kilroy then pronounced his shoulders up a little, cupped a hand around his mouth and began to whisper. "The big boy still has his days though, and on one of those days you don't want to be anywhere near him unless you have a 4x4. Last year when he was feeling particularly virile he tried to copulate with my wife's Honda Civic. Well I shouldn't say tried. There was irrevocable damage. I shan't make that mistake again gentlemen I assure you."

Buelfarbel twisted his head a little before speaking. "I didn't notice until now Kilroy, but are those ducks blind?" The men watched two of them bump into each other and simultaneously quack. Another one just kept bumping into the wall.

"The ducks and the chickens, although they're purblind, which means they can see shapes and such. It's a harrowing story. They all lived together in the backyard of a house not too far from the farm. One day about five months ago there was a great explosion, I remember I was icing down my hands after milking Bessie and Bessie when I heard it. The kind of explosion that rattles your bones men." Kilroy instinctively began shaking his hands when his eyes suddenly grew wide. "Apparently a piece of space debris by means of orbital decay hurtled down from a low earth orbit and into the propane tank in the rear of the house and blew it to smithereens. Fortunately no one was home, but the chickens and the ducks that were not laid waste by the shrapnel were blinded from the flash of the explosion. They were naturally assumed deceased and forgotten until a few days later when an avid golfer with a putting green in his backyard found them trying to incubate his practice balls. He tried to shoo the fowl from the premises with his pitching wedge but they put up a fight thinking they were protecting their eggs. The man recalled to me that it was quite the skirmish. Strength in numbers I remember him saying."

"And Gamble can herd them into the henhouse," Davenport asked.

"All twenty of them. I told you he's a smart one. No doubt you can tell when he's at work. With the chickens, ducks, and Gamble it sounds like some sort of primitive steam engine. It's actually quite soothing."

"So that brings us to the lemur."

"You're correct Mr. Davenport, a ring-tailed lemur. Burgle was C.B.'s favorite. He's a mischievous little scapegrace with a mind particularly designed to obtain eyeglasses. He was a resident of the zoo here in town until his kleptomaniacal tendencies got the best of him. Unbeknownst to the staff, Burgle had been pilfering spectacles for more than five years. The way in which they found out about Burgle's affliction was somewhat by happenstance. A staff member caught the primate red-handed trying to help himself to a pair of sun cheaters worn by an elderly gentleman who walked too close to the enclosure. The zookeeper then proceeded to try to catch Burgle and win back the eyewear but she was no match for his deftness of limb. Apparently she pulled a hamstring in the attempted apprehension of Burgle and went down in a heap next to a curious mound of earth. The woman then saw a slight play of light coming from the accumulation of soil whist prostrate and did an impromptu investigation." Kilroy paused and shook his head disapprovingly.

"She had found Burgle's hoard and he was less than pleased. He immediately went into hysterics and began urinating on the hapless employee, presumably to mark the cache as his own, finally chasing the hopping keeper from the enclosure. The result was an intensive excavation that lasted the better part of an hour. Fifty-seven gentlemen," Kilroy said with a satisfied smile.

"Amazing," said Buelfarbel.

Davenport raised an eyebrow. "Didn't the zoo receive complaints of stolen glasses by the patrons?"

"Of course, but what could they do? Burgle had made sure they were out of sight by the time the keepers came looking for them. When they uncovered the stash they then did an extensive categorization. It turns out Burgle was particularly adept at stealing monocles. The zoo put out a full page ad in the Sunday paper that week, asking people to come down if they had lost or had stolen any kind of eyepiece. Burgle wasn't

mentioned by name of course, and there was quite a showing…
mostly foreign dignitaries and third parties."

Davenport looked confused. "So how did Burgle wind
up in Dabney's possession?"

"Burgle became quite inconsolable after his ordeal and
lost a certain sense of himself. He was put under close surveil-
lance and was seen scavenging for anything he could find—
buttons, small denominations of currency, bits of refuse, but
nothing held the allure like the glasses. After a time he became
quite hostile toward the staff and his fellow lemurids. They
ultimately had to make the difficult decision and call the farm.
C.B. was more than happy to take Burgle. He has … he had me
wear fake glasses twice a week to keep the rapscallion in
operational condition. He was a beautiful man." Kilroy began to
weep softly for a moment but quickly pulled himself together.
He reached into the inside jacket pocket of his blazer and pulled
from it an embroidered kerchief, blew his nose with a mighty
honk and finished the job with a healthy side to side motion as if
he were swabbing the deck of a ship. The hanky was back in his
pocket within seconds. Both men offered their condolences.

"Thank you gentlemen. I do truly thank you."

Buelfarbel instinctively tried to change the subject. "So
what's wrong with the rooster?"

"Nothing's wrong with Alarmo," Kilroy said as he
started to well up again. "C.B. just loved cocks."

11:49

Davenport and Buelfarbel tried their best to console Kilroy with kind words and gentle pats on the back but it was obvious that he needed a little more than polite compassion. Davenport made the decision and gave the old-timer a hug. Kilroy immediately began gently sobbing onto Davenport's lapel.

"He was a good friend Davenport ... a good friend indeed. I shall miss him very much."

"I'm sorry Kilroy."

"Thank you Davenport," Kilroy said as he stood away from the embrace and collected himself, "I hope you can forgive my blubbering."

"Times of sorrow."

"Indeed." Kilroy reached into the front pocket of his shirt and pulled out a pair or reading glasses.

"Mr. Buelfarbel, could you?"

"Of course Kilroy," Buelfarbel said and took the glasses. He put them on and began walking warily around the room on the lookout for Burgle.

Davenport waited for Buelfarbel to be at a safe remove before he spoke. "Kilroy I'm afraid we need to have a frank discussion." He watched Kilroy shake his head with profound concern. It was a few moments before he responded.

"He was found in the altogether."

"Yes."

"And you have questions about the peanut butter."

"I do Kilroy."

"I see. Well I can be of some use as far as the peanut butter, and perhaps from my explanation we will be able to deduce C.B.'s state of undress."

"I want to show you something," Davenport said as he led Kilroy over to the window and pointed to the curtain. "I found this shortly after I arrived.

"Our friend Burgle."

"I suspected."

"This will make even more sense to you now. Ah Mr. Buelfarbel you've returned sans glasses. I thank you many times sir, and in the future many more."

"He's good, almost tactical."

"I was just about to explain to Mr. Davenport the reason for the peanut butter."

"Davenport do you mind if?"

"Please Buelfarbel."

"Truly excellent gentlemen to be sure. A more affable pair I have yet to encounter. Now as you know there was a reception for the swine here yesterday. Various photographs were taken to mark the occasion for posterity and also for C.B.'s private collection. Unbeknownst to many in and out of the clothing industry, C.B. was a recognized photographer in certain circles. The photographs of his animals were well received at state fairs across the country. Some would say this was because he required no monies for the pieces. If one knew him one would know better. The pictures he took yesterday were to be his masterworks. He had been training the animals for a solid six weeks, every day men, so he could get 'the shot' as he called it."

"The peanut butter was a training aid."

"Correct Mr. Davenport, and a very effective one at that. May I ask you both a question?"

Both men said certainly.

"What do you notice about the animals," Kilroy asked with a raised eyebrow. He noticed Buelfarbel's face scrunch up in bewilderment for a moment then pop back into place with the acquisition of the light going off in his head.

"Color."

"Exactly Mr. Buelfarbel."

Davenport shook his head. "Of course, they're either black or white or both."

"Astute young minds."

"So there was a particular arrangement. A pattern.

"Not just a pattern Mr. Davenport. A pattern that makes a picture."

"Black and white, like a Rorschach."

"Mr. Buelfarbel it seems as though you've done this before."

"Buelfarbel?"

"I'll explain later Davenport," Buelfarbel said and began looking around."

"You're looking for the camera."

"Yup."

"On the entrance wall twelve feet up," Kilroy said as he pointed a finger above the penthouse door. "A Hasselblad H4D-200MS mounted at a twenty-two degree angle with a shutter speed of one-six hundredth of a second if I remember correctly. The two flood lights on the ceiling were installed last week."

McMusker and Quinlap ... bastards didn't even look up, Davenport mumbled to himself. "We're gonna need a ladder," he said as he looked at the camera on the wall.

"There's an eight-foot step ladder in the hall closet next to the bathroom, I'll go ..."

"I'll get it Kilroy," said Buelfarbel.

"There should be a toolbox in there as well Mr. Buelfarbel."

"Okay."

"Should I tell you now or would you like to see for yourself Mr. Davenport."

"I would prefer to see for myself if you don't mind."

"Of course, then I shan't ruin the surprise."

"Kilroy?"

"Yes."

"Let's suppose C.B. had his clothes on when he fell."

"He told me he was going to wear a white linen suit and shirt and black loafers with no socks."

"Let's start with the loafers," Davenport said and the men began searching the room as Buelfarbel came back with the ladder and the tool box.

"What's up?"

"Looking for his shoes," Davenport said as he peeked behind a curtain.

"I'll get the camera." Buelfarbel set up the ladder, put the toolbox on the floor and opened it up.

"Any luck Kilroy?"

"None as of yet, no, wait … ah ha! Found one under the chesterfield Davenport."

"Clever Kilroy."

"A paltry bit of levity I'm afraid."

"What the hell is this," asked Davenport as he bent over and picked up what looked like a red sequined doily and showed it to Kilroy.

"Ah you've found Burgle's cowboy hat. Don't worry we have a box full at the farm."

"Up here's the other one, underneath Bessie or Bessie. Easy girl …" Davenport quickly retrieved the loafer, trying not to stare at Bessie's or Bessie's udders.

"You know guys I was thinking," said Buelfarbel as he stood on the ladder ratcheting a socket wrench, "I checked the security log for the penthouse and the first timestamp after we got the animals up here yesterday was this morning when I opened the door for Meltzman and Monfries. There was no activity in between. I really only see one possibility about the clothes."

Kilroy and Davenport had now gathered below the ladder. Kilroy took a moment to look at the loafer Davenport was holding. "Yours looks a little worse for wear."

"Yeah, heavier too. What are you thinking Buelfarbel?" Davenport dropped the shoe and grimaced at his hand. Buelfarbel looked over his shoulder down to the men. "They were eaten."

"Moist towelette?" Kilroy extended the toiletry to Davenport with a wink and a nod.

"Thanks Kilroy." Davenport opened the packaging and began to clean his hands. "So we know that Burgle had some-how gotten hold of the jar and peppered the room and the animals with peanut butter. Reason?"

"Imitation perhaps," said Kilroy. "He'd been watching C.B. train the animals with the spread for six weeks, plenty of time for that jackanapes to figure out its power."

Buelfarbel looked down to the men again. "The animals must have started to move from their designated positions."

"So Burgle got the peanut butter and was trying to get them back into position, in his own way of course," Davenport said as he paused for a moment. "Do we think Burgle tried to get C.B. in position, throwing peanut butter on him too?"

"If his clothes were covered with peanut butter," Buelfarbel said as he descended the ladder.

Kilroy threw up an index finger. "The goats men."

"Here it is." Buelfarbel handed the camera to Davenport.

"Thanks." Davenport took a moment to look at it. "Wait a minute. Where's the remote?"

"Oh crap you're right," said Buelfarbel, and the men started looking around the floor. It wasn't long before Kilroy found it, picked it up and produced another towelette and cleaned it off. Davenport turned his head slightly and closed an eye.

"So before we look at the pictures let's see if we have this straight. C.B. was swinging on the trapeze with his clothes on and somehow lost his grip and slipped and fell in a way that resulted in the breaking of his neck. The jar of peanut butter was somewhere, most certainly open. The animals started moving around and Burgle took it upon himself to try to correct the situation by throwing peanut butter everywhere. So far?"

"Yes."

"Yup."

"And after the peanut butter winds up all over C.B. the goats eat the clothes right off his back?" Davenport looked to Kilroy.

"Well it's quite possible that they all had a hand in it, so to speak. They had been trained to eat peanut butter and it had been over twenty-four hours since they had anything to eat, and we mustn't forget that his suit was basically plant material, most likely made from flax. Now that I think about it, I'm quite sure they all had to have eaten some. It had to have been done rather quickly though, for most of these animals will not eat tainted food, and Flora and Flavio were raised to be extremely hygienic." Kilroy concluded by raising his palms in the air.

"And this morning," asked Buelfarbel.

"You mean Meltzman." Davenport said as he looked around at the camera.

"Yeah."

"They were probably just taking care of the leftover peanut butter. Meltzman had no idea what we know. Now that I think about it, it could have been rather traumatic to witness such a thing ... wow."

"What?"

Davenport showed Buelfarbel the camera. They stood for a few moments scrolling through the pictures. Buelfarbel cocked his head to get a better look.

"They're beautiful."

"I told you he was good men."

"This is perfect," Davenport said, "I'll need to ..."

"I'm sure you'll return it unharmed."

"Buelfarbel how do you get the card ..."

"Here."

"No."

"Well now wait a minute."

"There it is. Okay Kilroy, the animals are free to go whenever you wish."

"I'll call a few of my men."

"There's one more thing I have to enter into evidence Kilroy. I feel horrible having to ask you this, but would you?"

"I'll find whatever comes out."

"Are you sure?"

"Wouldn't be the first time gentleman. I'll grab some Ziplocks from the kitchen," Kilroy said as he began to bend over. Buelfarbel and Davenport looked at each other. Buelfarbel cracked a smile. Davenport began to turn toward the door but stopped.

"You guys want to get a drink later?"

"Sure."

"Capital."

"I have to head to a debriefing then to the conference. How about around eight at the Blind Lady, its right around the corner."

"Fine with me," said Buelfarbel.

"That'll give me plenty of time to settle the animals back at the farm. Eight it is then."

"Thanks for everything Kilroy," Davenport said as he extended his hand, "truly indispensable."

"An accolade I'll take to my grave sir." The two men shook hands once again and Davenport felt a vigor in Kilroy's grip that seemed missing at their first meeting. Davenport mirrored Kilroy's confident nod of head and made his way to the door.

"I'll go with you Davenport. I want to make sure the loading dock is clear for Kilroy's trailers."

Both men said see ya Kilroy. He waved a hand without speaking as he was bent over immersed in the inspection of a cow pie.

BLATSKY & MAGGIE

"So what's with the getup Buelfarbel," Davenport asked as they waited for the freight elevator."

"It's Friday. My wife likes a man in uniform and I like to start the weekend off right."

"Makes sense."

"She still prefers the Justice blues though."

"So you have done this before. I don't remember a Buelfarbel and I've been with the department twenty years." Davenport stepped aside as Buelfarbel opened the gate to the elevator.

"I took my wife's surname after I left ... after I was forced to leave."

"What was ..."

"Chocko, Anton Chocko," Buelfarbel said as he closed the gate.

"You were the youngest Minister of Information ever

appointed."

"Until you."

"All I remember was hearing of your resignation and suddenly they bumped me up from Detectives. What the hell?"

"It was October 17, 2002. Mayor Carmine Blatsky had officially gone missing. His wife called Director Milton Clog personally when he failed to come home for two straight nights. Dunderhead's still there isn't he?"

"Unfortunatley."

"So Clog calls me into his office and starts in with his walking routine, telling me that this is the highest priority case we have pending and he wants me on it. Davenport I was giving interviews all day long back then, you know what it's like. I'd been out of Detectives for years. I was a little suspicious so I protested and he jammed a business card in my hand. He said Blatsky's wife found it underneath some Reader's Digests on the nightstand on his side of the bed. It read 'NineX Services' and underneath was a phone number and that was that. I was detecting again."

"Then what happened?"

"So I went back to my office and filed the paperwork to access his financial records. When I received clearance I found nothing out of the ordinary until I went down to the bank to get statements for the last couple days. Withdrawals from one of his accounts on October 15 and 16 totaled seventy-two hundred dollars, one for eighteen hundred and one for thirty-six hundred. Puzzled, I looked at his ATM activity on those two days. Even stranger. Every three or four hours he was taking out at least twenty bucks. Around the clock Davenport, I mean 11:30

P.M. twenty bucks, 2:30 A.M. thirty bucks, 7:00 A.M. twenty bucks for like forty-eight hours! All from an ATM on 2nd and Oak. Stymied I called the number." Buelfarbel reached for the lanyard that held his keys. He fumbled, found the right one, opened up the control box and shut down the elevator. He turned back around to Davenport with his hands out in front of his chest.

"I hear this husky female voice on the answering machine thanking me for calling NineX Services, but no one was available to take my call, etc. I hung up the phone and got some uniforms to knock on some doors around that corner and told them to ask the neighbors if they had seen anyone resembling the mayor around the area on those days. A few hours later the patrolmen got back to me. Almost everyone in the whole neighborhood had seen him at one time or another in the last three days. All reports had two things in common. He was always wearing a backpack and always in a hurry," Buelfarbel said as he raised an eyebrow.

"He was always in a hurry, little bastard."

"Exactly. So I do a search on the phone number and boom. 2nd and Oak. Crosse Apartments, Number 113. Well my interest is up at this point, so I head down there with the patrolmen and the detectives. We had the apartment opened by the super and almost everything becomes clear. NineX isn't just a service it's a person."

"How did you find that out?"

"She had 'NineX' tattooed on the small of her back and Davenport, I swear it was four feet wide if it was an inch. She was lying naked face down on her bed. Fast food bags, containers, soda cups and wrappers strewn all over the apartment but no Blatsky."

"Huh."

"Just wait. We had to call in some piano movers to get Ms. NineX down to the morgue. That's when we found him. NineX fell victim to a cardiac arrest. Blatsky fell victim to being in the wrong place at the wrong time … underneath her. Blatsky was a flesh fetishist who went on a bender and was apparently willing to pay by the pound."

"Thirty-six hundred and eighteen hundred. All divisible by nine hundred," said Davenport.

"Yup. Six times in forty-eight hours. I guess she didn't charge him to watch her eat, but she sure did charge him for the opportunity." Buelfarbel turned the elevator back on.

"So then what?"

"I went to Clog's office and gave him my report. He told me to bury it, told me to come up with some story, to cover it up. He was one of Blatsky's cronies, so I said okay and called a conference. I may be a lot of things but I'm no liar. It happened to a public official, so I let the public know. I was gone the next day. Clog gave a statement to the press that I had gone rogue because of some personal vendetta I had against Blatsky. The official cause of death became an aneurism. He died at home of course."

"That's funny."

"What?"

"Clog wants me to burn Dabney."

"He's up to something."

"I know." The elevator doors opened and the men stepped out.

"I'm going to see about the loading dock."

"Buelfarbel I think you should come with me."

"Down to Justice?"

"Yeah."

"Why?"

"I'll bring Clog to my office for the debriefing and you sneak into his office and see if you can dig anything up on him."

"I don't know if I can help Davenport. I've been out of the game ..."

"Well now you're back in."

2:36

Davenport stood leaning against the open car door. "Buelfarbel lose the coat and hat."

"Why?"

"Because you look like a third world dictator when you're not in the hotel. You're out of context."

"I suppose you're right." Buelfarbel shimmied off his coat and took off his hat. He threw both onto the front passenger seat and they slammed their doors in unison and began walking through the lower levels of the parking garage toward the elevators. Both sensed a mild enormity, a feeling that caused them to synchronize their gaits as if marching toward some imperiled cause. They both stepped into the elevator. It was a mere thirty-seven floors to The Office of Justice, but as the men looked at each other while ascending it was taking too long. Davenport made a bid to level Buelfarbel's nerves.

"So you just wear the hat on Fridays too?"

"Yup. I'm in a suit and tie most of the week."

"You have any kids?"

"No. Linda and I decided early on that it wasn't really for us."

"My wife's name's Linda."

"No kidding?" said Buelfarbel.

"Yup. We have a son, Giles Jr. We had him pretty young. He's twenty-seven and strangely enough works in the hotel restaurant business."

"Is that right."

"He and his wife run a B&B out in the country."

"Nice. Any grandkids?"

"Not yet," Davenport said as he leaned against the elevator wall. He rolled his eyes to himself, being a little wary of moving in a personal direction. "How long have you and Linda been married?"

"This year'll be … twenty-six, no seven, twenty-seven. You?"

"Tomorrow night's our twenty-fifth. So how do you keep it going Buelfarbel, besides the getup on Fridays?"

"The latest kinda happened just because of life. Linda is a few years younger than I am, and about a year and a half ago she started having some urinary incontinence issues, you know sneezing and laughing a little would come out. So she went to see her gynecologist and the prescription was kegel exercises and Ben Wa balls."

"Really?"

"Yup. They both strengthen the PC muscle and help with bladder control and vaginal elasticity, among other things."

"Is that so."

"Yup. She started with 3/4" balls in the beginning, now she's up to 1 1/4". I love my wife Davenport, so I don't mind telling you she could rip the door knob off a door if she wanted to. I swear sometimes I feel like somebody's in there trying to reel me in like a tuna."

"Congratulations," said Davenport and extended a hand.

"Thank you," said Buelfarbel and shook it.

"My wife's been bugging me for a while to try something new, but I've been a little apprehensive, it just hasn't seemed like …"

"We're here," Buelfarbel said, "sorry … habit."

"Shit that reminds me," Davenport reached into his pants pocket and gave Buelfarbel his card. "Call my cell so I'll have your number. Hang out in the lobby till you see me walk to my office with Clog, then sneak into his office and poke around. I'll text you when he leaves my office. We'll meet back at the car."

"Is Clog still in the same office?"

"Yup. It's like riding a bike Anton."

"Fucking Clog," Buelfarbel said as he made his way to the reception area. Davenport began making mental notes about the jabs he was going to take at the reporters during the conference as he winked and nodded his way through the office. He stopped in front of Clog's assistant's desk. "Hi Marie, is Clog?" Davenport ticked his head toward the office door.

"He's in there, but watch it Giles," she said as she cupped a hand around the side of her mouth, "I walked in there fifteen minutes ago and he was doing deep knee bends."

"No squat thrusts?"

"Not yet."

"Then we're safe for now." Davenport smiled and knocked on the door. "It's Davenport."

"Come in dammit!"

Oh crap he's doing squat thrusts, Davenport thought as he closed the door. "Just got back from the scene."

"How's it looking?" The Director stood erect and found the handkerchief in his back pocket. He began dabbing his face and neck haphazardly.

"Jesus Milt, it's gotta be a hundred degrees in here," Davenport said as he pulled on the collar of his shirt.

"One hundred four to be exact. I've invented Bikram calisthenics."

Davenport just shook his head. "Do you mind if we walk and talk? I have to get to my computer and put a couple things together for the conference."

"Of course," said the Director as he looked at his watch. "I'm doing the simulation of the climbing of Mt. Everest this week, so your office may just take me to through The Western Cwm." The Director produced a smile that expected congratulation. Davenport took a step back from the ridiculous aura of the Director's self-satisfaction. Davenport thought what a fucking douchewhistle.

"Do you plan to summit with or without oxygen sir," Davenport asked with a straight face. The Director looked at him quizzically, not sure if he was being used as the butt of a joke or if it was just a gentle ribbing. Either way he decided to be offended.

"With or without ox …" he said with a look of disgust,

"Does it look like we're in the goddamn Himalayas ... Well does it?"

Davenport shrugged.

The Director looked up confidently from his tie and began smoothing it out with his hand. "Although I will be wearing an altitude training mask all tomorrow morning." The Director tightened the knot of his tie and walked toward the door. "They're not for the faint of heart."

"Of course not," said Davenport as he held the door open and followed the Director through the doorway. "By the way I think it would be a good idea if Marie joined us." Davenport stopped in front of Marie's desk. "There may be a few things you'll want her to jot down, rather scandalous I'm afraid." Davenport watched the Director begin to rub his hands together as if he were about to receive a long awaited treat.

"Excellent! What did I tell you Davenport! Marie come with us please we're off to Davenport's office. This morning I told you didn't I Davenport," said the Director as he began walking at a brisk pace. He suddenly threw up an index finger. "A fine day, a fine day indeed. And to think I'm on pace to summit tomorrow noon. Just wonderful."

Davenport glanced over to Buelfarbel who looked up at him from a periodical. They both nodded. Davenport shook his head and rolled his eyes. Buelfarbel waited until they were out of sight then made his way to Clog's office.

Once inside, Buelfarbel went to Clog's desk and sat down in his chair. Jesus Christ it's hot in here, he thought as looked around the desk and found a legal pad marked by various calisthenics with repetitions and corresponding altitudes. After a few ridiculous smirks Buelfarbel decided to move on but stopped when he saw *Sell DPLUS* written and circled on the top right corner of the pad. Buelfarbel pulled out his phone and after a few seconds found that DPLUS was the stock designation for Dabney Plus-Size Baby Clothes Corporation. Buelfarbel shook his head and snatched a tissue from the box before he put his hand on the mouse. In a few seconds everything was illuminated. It took Buelfarbel a couple minutes to navigate through the etrading platform, but it wasn't long before he knew exactly what had occurred and what was soon to become. It was too good to be true and Buelfarbel noticed the Director's email was open as well.

===================

"I thought you said there was scandal here Davenport," said the Director with a mystified look on his face as he stood in front of Davenport's desk. "There's nothing but fanciful tales of pitiful farm animals and a dog that fart-barks. What the hell is going on!"

"I thought the fifty-seven pairs of glasses pretty impressive." Davenport then saw a slight nervousness in the legs of the Director. Lunges? No standing side leg lifts. He was wrong on both accounts as he watched the Director slowly lower himself into a squat. "Ah the duck walk," Davenport said as he watched the Director waddle around his office.

"This cannot stand Davenport!"

"What do you mean?

"There was peanut butter at the scene goddammit!"

"It was a training aid."

"I'll bet it was that sick son of a ..."

"For the pictures Milt. He was taking pictures."

"Good God!" said the Director heavily. "Where are they?"

"They're being processed as we speak. I saw them all Milt, there's nothing of a sexual nature whatsoever." Davenport looked at the memory card that was still in his computer.

"Then where the hell are his clothes Davenport!" The Director half yelled and half grunted as he stood up. "Can you at least tell me that?

"They ate them."

"What?"

"We figured his clothes must have been covered in peanut butter and the animals were hungry. It was a linen suit sir."

"A linen suit … Well then there it is," the Director said with an incredulous smile. "What's next Davenport, we bring 'em all downtown, interrogate them and watch as they crap all over the floor! No no you could be right Davenport the monkey could give us something vital … Godammit! Marie get McMusker and Quinlap in here on the double." The Director watched as Marie got up and left. "Their sheet is your sheet Davenport. I can't listen to any more cockamamie stories. Ziempa's going to handle the press for this one."

"Milt I'm not sure you're under . . ." Davenport knew he was going to get cut off, so he spent the time emailing himself the photos.

"Understand what Davenport? That you're off your ass?" the Director suddenly stopped and looked at his wrist. "How could I still be in the valley of silence … I've been duck walking for … high altitude bullshit! We're not finished here Davenport!" The Director immediately sat down, put his hands behind him and lifted himself off the floor on his hands and feet. He started crab-walking back to his office.

"Jeeze he's really moving," said Davenport as he popped out of his chair, reached for his cell phone and made his way to the door. He had his thumb on send when his cell inexplicably bounced out of his hand. All he saw was stomach.

"You dropped something," said McMusker as he stood in the doorway.

"Will there ever come a day when your belly doesn't precede you Dan." Davenport simultaneously picked up his phone and tried to squeeze through a gap between McMusker's fat and the door jam. He couldn't make it. He took a step backward and checked the phone. He hadn't sent the text. Davenport closed one eye as he pressed send because the Director was coming in hot.

━━━━━━━━━━━━━━━━━━━━━

Buelfarbel was a flurry expanding and collapsing windows, printing documents and sending emails. As he wiped the sweat from his forehead he remembered he hadn't been this busy since last year's International IBSD Convention. Flashes of the hotel buzzing with people that needed things done immediately but couldn't stay until their completion filled his mind. There were the sweaty brows—the nervous, controlled movements—the vulnerable please sympathize with me glances. Some needed multiple visits to check in. The porters were running around the lobby like it were a field hospital, creating an ad hoc triage unit for the luggage of the incontinent.

Brevity was at a premium, as well as eye-hand coordination. He couldn't remember how many ten-yard key card passes he made to people with their butt cheeks clenched shuffling desperately to the bathroom. Suddenly there was a text message alert, and Buelfarbel jumped out of the chair and collected the paper from the printer. He quickly arranged the chair back in position and checked the computer one more time. His eyes widened as he wiped down the keyboard and heard the Director's voice in the hallway.

━━━━━━━━━━━━━━━━━━━━━

Davenport stood in his office waiting for McMusker to get out of the way.

"Dan get out of the way."

"Make me," chuckled McMusker.

"What are we twelve?"

"Marie said the Director wanted me and Quinlap in your office. Quinlap's dropping a deuce. Where is he anyway?"

"He went crabbing out of here a second ago. Now get the hell out of the way you tubba guts, I gotta talk to him again." Davenport gave McMusker a shove.

"When was the last time you said something nice to me Davenport," McMusker asked with a smile.

"I don't know Dan, when was the last time you found your pecker with your eyes?" Davenport made it through the doorway and began walking down the hall.

"Bannon Jascoe Davenport!" said McMusker as he leaned into the hallway and smiled.

"Up yours Jabba!" Davenport threw the finger over his shoulder and kept it there as he began to walk faster.

"Hey why … Davenport? Davenport!" McMusker's face straightened when Davenport looked back at him and began walking even faster. It took a few seconds but Dan eventually started rumbling down the hallway.

▬▬▬▬▬▬▬▬▬▬▬▬▬▬▬▬▬▬▬▬

Even though Buelfarbel knew there was only one way out of the office he instinctually turned to each side of the office in a rapid succession of futile maneuvers, finally spying the waste paper basket next to the desk. He threw the paper in the basket and picked it up just as the Director came into the room. He was still walking backwards on his hands and feet and he didn't see Buelfarbel.

"Trash day sir," Buelfarbel said in a low voice.

"Is that you Dutch? I thought you'd be at home after that groin injury during *Buns of Steel* this morning … Dutch?" The Director looked over his right shoulder and Buelfarbel hopped left, then he looked over his left shoulder and Buelfarbel hopped right. This went on a few more times.

"Who the hell … goddammit who's in here!"

"Anton Chocko."

▬▬▬▬▬▬▬▬▬▬▬▬▬▬▬▬▬▬▬▬

Shit he's still in there, thought Davenport as he came to the Director's office. He suddenly remembered McMusker and turned his head toward the hallway. Dan rounded the corner and Davenport repeatedly pushed both palms down toward the ground. "Slow down," he whispered.

"Can't!" bellowed McMusker.

"What do you mean can't?"

"I'll pull … somethin' … you gotta … do it …"

"All right all right," said Davenport as he prepared

himself for 'The Dan Maneuver,' originally employed at the Department picnic three years ago when McMusker slipped out of a swing and was sent hurtling toward the kids' finger painting table. He was on a collision course to mush about a half dozen toddlers so Davenport dropped his funnelcake and ran after him. About six feet from a table full of wide-eyed little squirts Davenport made the beginning of a perfect form tackle and exploded into McMusker but failed to wrap up his tremendous girth and bounced off him and landed on the ground. The impact was so intense that it changed Dan's trajectory completely. Traveling backwards, McMusker was desperately trying to keep his legs under him as he flailed down a small hill, finally falling over a dinosaur spring rider and wedging himself underneath a merry-go-round. Davenport looked up and noticed a couple tots pondering clapping, one painting her smock and another with a look of consternation, most likely laying down the law in his huggies.

"Are ... ready ..."

"Here we go big boy!" Davenport was suddenly hypnotized by the directions in which McMusker's flesh was moving underneath his strained button down shirt. It was like if one of those buttons failed, it could cause a chain reaction and Dan would likely spill out all over the hallway rug. Davenport quickly shook it off, got himself into the break-down position and began concentrating solely on McMusker's hips. Time seemed to slow. He felt the vibrations grow more and more intense with each foot-fall. At the top of his field of vision Davenport saw McMusker's tits begin to roll slowly from side to side in tandem with his belly. Davenport calculated one more step, and he crouched down for a split second before delivering a devastating hip-check that sent them staggering into Clog's office. Their feet got tangled up and Davenport wound up falling on top of McMusker, bouncing off him then falling to the floor. Both men shook their heads for a second, then looked up and saw Clog and Buelfarbel choking each other.

"Is that the bellhop," asked McMusker.

"Jesus Christ." Davenport got up as quickly as he could and made his way in between them.

"Ruin my career for that little …"

"Anton … An …"

"Ever bother to go to her funeral?"

"I didn't … have … the address."

"Name was Margaret Mahue."

"I didn't …"

"Friends called her Big Maggie."

"It was … a tragedy," the Director gurgled.

"Gave to fifteen charities monthly you mother …"

"All right guys!" Davenport said as he jostled in between them. McMusker finally got up and helped Davenport separate the two. Clog and Buelfarbel stood hunched over and breathing heavily. With one hand on a hip Clog pointed to the door.

"Get him … the hell out of here!" The Director said breathlessly, wagging his index finger to solidify his command. Buelfarbel stood up straight.

"Check your trash can Milt," Buelfarbel said as he made his way to the door.

"And you Davenport, consider yourself on leave!"

Davenport shrugged. Both men walked out of Clog's

office into the hallway. Davenport turned to Buelfarbel as they walked down the hallway.

"You find anything?"

"Plenty. Check your email," said Buelfarbel as they made it to the elevator. Buelfarbel pushed the down button and looked over to Davenport who was looking at his phone. He started smiling. The door opened and both men walked into the empty elevator.

"This is good Anton."

"He's not walking away from this one without at least a ball missing." Buelfarbel began calming himself down by tucking in his shirt and straightening his tie. "What are you doing now," he asked as the elevator door closed.

"Sending out a press release for the conference. Can we do it at the hotel?"

"Sure, none of our conference rooms are booked, but aren't you on leave?"

"The press doesn't know that."

"They're not going to care either. Thanks Giles, by the way. I feel twenty years younger. Thanks for bringing me in on this."

"You deserve it Anton," said Davenport and the men shook hands. "You hungry?"

"Hell yeah we haven't eaten all day."

"Good I know a place on the way."

"I wonder if Kilroy found any evidence," said Buelfarbel.

"Crap I forgot about Kilroy." Davenport reached into his pocket for his phone.

"What he found or didn't find could be the clincher," said Buelfarbel.

"We're right Anton, I know it. There's no way ... hey Kilroy it's Davenport ... you did? Great, thanks again for doing that, I know it was ... yeah I know but ... well thanks just the same Kilroy. We couldn't have done this without you. Yeah Buelfarbel and I are going to grab something to eat before we head back over to the hotel for the conference. Okay then we'll see you back in town around eight ... yup The Blind Lady ... okay then ... see you there ... bye."

"Well?"

"Said he's bagged and tagged enough material for definitive proof. It's what happened Anton."

"Kilroy's the man."

"Yeah he is." The elevator door opened and the men walked out into the parking garage.

THE CONFERENCE

Davenport stood behind the lectern putting together the Powerpoint for the conference. He shook his head, not quite sure if he should show what he had on the reporters, but what the hell, he thought, this was his last day at Justice anyway. He decided that he'd keep them in because he knew those two idiots not only were going to ask the dumbest questions, but because they quite frankly deserved it. He knew they were going to make a mockery of a person that he had never known but had grown quite aware was a good person. Davenport stopped for a second and stood thinking of that word—Good. C.B. Dabney was a good man, by all accounts a solid human being that cared more for others than he cared for himself. He could have lived a fuck you lifestyle, but he chose to raise pigs for competition and save unwanted animals. Yup, he decided he was going to demoralize Billings and Raybach.

When he finished inserting all the photos he looked up

and Buelfarbel had just walked in the room. He stopped and talked to a couple workers setting up the chairs before he made his way over.

"Everything okay Davenport?"

"Yup, just finished the Powerpoint. What's up?"

"I'm having my guys bring in some more chairs. It looks like this is going to be a big one Giles." Buelfarbel looked at his watch. "You wanted this to go off around six right?"

"Yeah that's what I said in the release, but we usually make them wait a little extra."

"All right. We have about forty-five minutes." Buelfarbel looked over as the men were bringing in more chairs. "You know Clog's going to figure it out when nobody shows up over there."

"He'll put two and two together. I'll have a little surprise for him if he actually shows up. Since we have some time Anton, let's head up to the penthouse. There's something I want to check out.

"Okay I'll be right behind you, I just need to check on a few things."

Davenport nodded his head and made his way to the elevators. His phone buzzed a text message alert in his pocket and he took it out. "Jesus," Davenport said to himself, "she won't quit." He put the phone back in his pocket and looked up at the ceiling. The thought of it in and of itself wasn't too bad but it was the fact of how much she wanted to try it that made him a little queasy. He pulled his phone back out and sent her three ellipses. That'll hold her off for a couple hours, thought Davenport. Just as he slid the phone back in his pants pocket the elevator door opened. Davenport stepped out and made his way through the anteroom and into the penthouse. The place still smelled like the animals were all still in here, and he had a strange sense of nostalgia now that they were gone. It just happened this morning, but as he walked around he felt somehow disassociated from the experience. Maybe because the whole thing had been so damn interesting. He felt bad for C.B. and felt guilty that he had so much fun today. But he was here on business, and he walked over to the ladder that was still next to the front wall and picked it up. He walked it over and placed it underneath the trapeze. He climbed up to the second to last step.

"What are you thinking Giles?" Buelfarbel said as he walked through the door.

"I didn't want to think anything Anton, but I had a suspicion when we found the remote this morning," said Davenport as he inspected the chains. About two feet up from the bar on the right hand side he found it.

"What is it?"

"Peanut butter smeared on five links of chain."

"That's how he slipped? Burgle must have thrown it sometime in between some of the pictures."

"When we were scrolling through the pictures, Burgle and Gamble weren't in some of them." Davenport looked at the chain and sighed.

"Kilroy's going to take this hard Davenport."

"There's nothing on the other chain, just this one. I bet he was holding onto the chain with his left as he was taking pictures with his right. Burgle must have hit the chain with a glob at some point and when C.B. put his hand on the wrong spot with the remote still in his hand he lost his grip." Davenport shook his head and climbed back down the ladder.

"What are we going to tell him Davenport," Buelfarbel asked as he looked to the ground.

"We don't have to tell him anything Anton. What's the point? It was an accident either way." Davenport walked over to the bathroom and grabbed a towel.

"Do you think he knows?"

"Who Burgle?"

"Yeah."

"I don't know, but he did hide from Kilroy this morning." Davenport climbed back up the ladder and began to clean the peanut butter from the chain.

"What a damn shame Davenport."

"I know Anton," he said as he descended the ladder. "I'm so used to finding out the ugly truth. This one was all about beauty. I wish I knew him."

"Me too. I think you have to be someone like Kilroy to know somebody like Dabney. He gets it, the underneath of things." Buelfarbel looked around the room. "I'll have the whole cleaning crew in here tomorrow. "We'll fix it up like new and seal it off."

"What time is it Anton?"

"Quarter till six"

"All right. Let's get down there and let 'em have it."

━━━━━━━━━━━━━━━━━━━━

The Director walked into the conference room and saw a lone Ziempa looking at one of his index fingers and concluded he had just been picking his nose. He rolled his eyes and refrained from smoothing out his tie. "Use a goddamn Kleenex Ziempa! Have a little respect for the Office for Christ's sake … Where the hell is everybody?"

"Yes sir." Ziempa reached over for the box of Kleenex and knocked it over. "Sorry sir," Ziempa moaned as he bent over, "it was supposed to start at five thirty. I don't know …" Ziempa looked to a corner of the room as he indiscreetly cleaned off the offending finger.

"Be in my office in five minutes with an answer Ziempa! And you'd better spend some of that time washing your hands!" Milt walked out of the room satisfied with the modicum of fear he had just instilled in Ziempa, but if he was being honest with himself Burt was truly to blame. That goddamn son of a bitch, thought the Director, but then he suddenly realized it wasn't an insult, so that just made his hate for the canine that much more visceral. He rounded the corner to his office and sat down in his chair. He took two deep breaths and pulled out his phone.

"Goddamn butt-sniffer's half way up the Lhoste Face," the Director growled. "Well I'll fix him," and Milt pulled out of his desk drawer what he called "The Howitzer," a 16oz bottle of energy gel and began chugging it. He grimaced as he gulped down the foul tasting goo and finished the whole thing as Ziempa walked into his office. He gagged a little as he wiped his mouth with his shirtsleeve.

"What did you find out Ziempa!" he bellowed as he stood up and moved away from his desk and started doing squat thrusts.

"Davenport's having the press conference at Dabney's

hotel sir."

"What?"

"Davenport's having the press ..."

"I heard you goddammit! When?"

"At six sir."

"That son of a bitch," grunted the Director as he stood up. "What did Chocko say ..."

"Sir?"

"Said check ..." and Milt looked over to the trash can. He walked over and snatched the paper out of it. The color drained from his face as he shuffled the papers. "All right," he said as he reached into the drawer and grabbed his training mask. "Let's go."

"Sir?"

"Two birds with one stone, that's how I fucking like to do things Ziempa. Follow me," and the Director walked out of the office. Ziempa looked confused when they walked by the elevator.

"Sir the elevator is over ..."

"I know where the Christ the elevator is Ziempa! We're taking the stairs! Get the shit out of your ears Ziempa you could use the exercise." The Director stood up straight and put on the mask.

"Yes sir." Ziempa lowered his head and followed Director to the stairwell. As they descended the building Ziempa was falling farther and farther behind, and every so often he'd look down and see the Director flailing his arms and hopping up and down waiting for him to catch up. Ziempa couldn't understand a word he was saying, so he just resorted to saying yes sir every thirty seconds or so.

By the time they were outside Ziempa was exhausted, and he stopped at the corner to wait for a cab.

"Were olking"

"Excuse me sir?"

"Were olking!"

"What?"

The Director ripped off the mask. "We're walking Ziempa goddammit!"

"It's got to be twenty blocks sir!"

"This is no time to stand around Ziempa!" Milton then put the mask back on and started speed walking. Ziempa made a bitchy face as he kicked the ground and begrudgingly stumbled after him. A few minutes passed and Milt looked behind him and Ziempa was about a half a block away breathing heavily. The Director pulled out his phone and found that he and Burt had passed the Yellow Band and were heading for the Geneva Spur. The Director looked up and suddenly realized he was in surroundings he didn't recognize. A thin shiver of panic crept up the Director's back and he froze. The unfamiliar territory held him to the sidewalk like a magnet, and he looked around at the strange new world and felt tiny and alone. Ziempa was his only hope. He pretended he was waiting for him but what he truly needed was for someone to hold his hand. As soon as Ziempa was close enough the Director grabbed his hand and began dragging him down the sidewalk toward the hotel. God knows what the fellow pedestrians thought seeing a masked man in a suit dragging a pudgy man in his twenties down the street …

==========================

The place was packed, and the anticipation in the room was as palpable as a slobbering dog waiting for a snausage. As Davenport walked up to the podium he noticed the familiar commotion of the reporters and he felt faintly transposed in time. For a moment his mind shot him back to this morning outside the penthouse door. The only difference, Davenport thought, was what was being transmitted through the air. This time all he could sniff out was all the potential bullshit. It didn't take long for Davenport to find Billings and Raybach, they were both up front. He could see the excitement in their eyes and they were squirming in their seats like a couple of kindergarteners right before recess. Davenport kept his contemptuous smile behind the one that greeted the reporters. He waited a couple more seconds for the room to quiet.

"At approximately five o'clock this morning the Office of Justice received ..." and he was off. Davenport explained the noise complaint from the penthouse, the call from the night manager and the eventual opening of the penthouse door. He went on to provide the reporters with the state of C.B. Dabney and the approximate time of death. He then explained that all thirty-five of the patrolmen were fine and all had been discharged from the hospitals. It was when he began to explain the various animals in the penthouse and some of the wedding attire that he heard a few snickers. When he mentioned the trapeze it turned to subdued chuckles. The open laughter came when he disclosed the peanut butter at the scene, and all hell broke loose when he mentioned the camera. Davenport waited patiently for the conference room to settle down and looked over to Joe Billings and Samantha Raybach who were both wiping tears from their eyes. To be fair there were many in the audience that were taking their jobs and the situation seriously, and Davenport knew they were C.B.'s only hope in having some respect amid this unfortunate event.

Davenport started with the investigation itself. The corroboration of the training and the pictures by the farm manager Kilroy Fuss. Incredulous looks abounded by those who thought it unbelievable that the linen suit was consumed by the livestock, even when Davenport told them of the evidence collected at the scene. The validity of the theory put forth about Burgle and the peanut butter flew in the face of some that thought it truly unreasonable, and Davenport saw more than a few reporters roll their eyes. Finally, the time and place where C.B.'s mortal remains were located was divulged. Davenport prepared himself for the ridiculousness that was about to commence.

"I'll now answer a few questions."

"..." (inaudible)

"No Joe, absolutely no top hats were on the scene. Next question."

"..." (inaudible)

"Do you think a hoof can hold a cane? No. None were found. Next.

"..." (inaudible)

"Yes Cleland Dabney was the only surviving heir to the Dabney Plus-size Baby Clothes Corporation."

"..." (inaudible)

"At this time chunky or creamy is irrelevant Samantha. Yes go ahead."

"…" (inaudible)

"Really? No there was no bachelor party that we know of."

"…" (inaudible)

"No originally Mr. Dabney's farm was only being used to raise Chester White pigs for competition. It was only after a series of unfortunate incidents that the farm became a shelter for unwanted animals."

"…" (inaudible)

"Yes all the animals in the penthouse except the two Chester Whites were taken in by Dabney."

"…" (inaudible)

"Yes Dabney was a noted animal photographer. Some of his photographs were widely circulated in various husbandry magazines and also at state fairs across the country." Davenport cleared his throat before he continued. "That leads me to the pictures from the scene. I'd like to show you what Dabney was actually doing in the penthouse at the time of his death. I feel that I must do this to put to rest the ridiculous conjecture that has been floated about since this morning." Davenport reached for the glass of water on the shelf of the podium and took a sip.

"When news of this tragedy first began to circulate within our own office, it was the lack of factual evidence that sent thirty-five men and women from the Office of Justice to the emergency room with various wounds sustained from hot coffee. Minds begin to go to strange places without facts, and those men and women certainly allowed their imaginations to get the better of them. When the scant information was then leaked to various news organizations and then to social media a man's life and legacy was put into question with no regard for the truth. I've put forth the truth today, and I will not allow conjecture to destroy a man that cannot defend himself. That is why I'm going to release this picture to the public, but before I do I'd like to take a moment to single out two reporters that are at the heart of the problem. Joe Billings and Samantha Raybach. The questions you put forth this evening lack the professional integrity and respect for the truth that should be in the hearts of all journalists. One shouldn't be judged by speculation and assumption, nor should one be held accountable for one's entire life because of one indiscretion. Now Samantha and Joe think it's funny to make wild presumptions about a defenseless man with absolutely no evidence. I have a little evidence of my own. I sent a letter of resignation to Director Milton Cog and hour and a half ago after being put on leave, so my last news conference, this one, right now isn't even official." Davenport listened to the murmurs of the crowd and waited an extra couple seconds to let the tension build before he went on.

"One night two years ago at the correspondents' dinner here in town a series of events lead to a picture. It was never known to the subject, as the taker of the picture, a competitor, sent it to me as a joke because over the years she knew the way in which the person conducted herself professionally, and the countless inappropriate questions I had to deal with over the years. This person had the decency not to post it to social media, but I fear I don't have the same amount of restraint." Davenport clicked the mouse and he immediately heard several gasps, followed by a dim wave of whispers. Davenport opened his arm to the screen to his left.

"The vomit on the table, for those of you with good memories looks vaguely like the chicken Kiev served that evening. Luckily her face was kept out of the mess due to her tits being wedged in a couple of martini glasses. And yes, unfortunately her white pantsuit had been sullied by the telltale shart, poor Samantha." Davenport looked down to Raybach and she had her hands over her face. Billings was looking nervous.

"And Joe Billings, one of a long line of idiots that can't tell the difference between reply and reply all," Davenport said as he clicked the mouse again and pointed to the picture. "Apparently there was an interoffice 'Testicle Olympics' where the contestants took pictures of their reproductive organs and were judged on difficulty and creativity, luckily for Joe size wasn't a category. Looks like a couple pieces of gum fell onto a dust bunny. That seemingly benign click sent his picture, and the email thread of other nuts all over the office, hence the reason why Joe is currently working at the rag he is. Oh yeah and in college he was really good at being caught screwing fruit." Davenport clicked through the pictures and heard the guffaws and cackles as they showed Joe in various states of surprise while in various melons—cantaloupe, honey dew, casaba.

"You'll know for next time Billings," Davenport said as he watched him stomp out of the room. At least Raybach had the balls to sit there and take it, thought Davenport. He clicked to the next picture in the Powerpoint and the room went dead silent.

Because it was so damn good. C.B. was in the bottom right corner of the frame swinging up toward the lens with a devilish grin. Because of the angle of the camera on the wall, above his shoulder was the alpha and omega of the whole chain of events. Worker was the mouth, positioned in such a way as to create a broad and happy smile. Flora and Flavio were the plump cheeks. Bessie's and Bessie's black patches were arranged to make the eyes and the white patches created more of the face. The goats were positioned around the pigs to create dimples and freckles. The chickens were the forehead, and the ones speckled with black furrowed the brow to increase its animation. The ducks were dispersed to fill out the smiley face's roundness and purpose. Alarmo the rooster was at the bottom of the face and created a subtle cleft chin. At the bottom of the picture Gamble was high in the air catching a Frisbee with Burgle in the saddle waving his cowboy hat like he was bronco bucking.

The contrast of the black and white on the parquet floor made the face even more three dimensional, and the lights from the ceiling created a soft shadow around the edges of the animals. The sun beamed huge diagonal columns of light into the room, making the picture look even more majestic and ethereal. The picture was so vivid and quirky and beautiful that even Davenport himself stood mesmerized at the foot of C.B.'s achievement. It was the first time he had ever felt proud of a man he had never known.

And yet the silence in the room also held a weight of humility. The photo showed those in the room that their minds were the perpetrators of innuendo and culprits to the perversions of the truth. There was silence because they themselves had made the darkness and now it had been extinguished by the light. Suddenly the conference room doors burst open and the audience collectively turned their heads to the back of the room. The Director stood tall and rather imposing as he still wore the training mask. Ziempa stood next to him white in the face and panting with a huge bib of sweat on his shirt. The Director began talking and flailing his arms.

"They can't hear you you fucking idiot," Ziempa said breathlessly before his eyes rolled into the back of his head and he passed out and fell to the floor. The Director ripped off the mask and pointed his finger at Davenport.

"This made is a liar and a fraud!" said the Director as he walked down the aisle toward Davenport. "He is no longer Minister of Information, no longer part of the investigation and no longer employed by the Office of Justice! This is unofficial!" the Director himself seemed surprised by how high-pitched his voice became. He looked up to Davenport, who had his index finger pointed down to the podium as if one jab of his finger could spiral the Director's life out of control. Milt slowed down. "Now Davenport …"

"You tell them or I'll show them."

"I have no idea …" Davenport moved his hand down a little.

"Giles, Giles now wait a …"

He moved his hand down a little closer and cocked his head.

"Goddammit Davenport! Just hold on a second now. Just a second now hold on," said the Director as he raised his arms slightly. He took a few more steps and leaned into Davenport and lowered his voice. He looked like a man tipping on the edge of something massive. His eyes darted around his face like he was having several conversations at the same time.

"Let's talk about this Giles, I'm sure you ..." The Director's phone began ringing and he reached into his pocket and pulled it out. "Damn you Burt," said the Director and he began to sob. The weight of the race and his indiscretions had finally caught up to him, and his body had begun to dictate his mind. "Fine Davenport, goddammit fine. I did it!" he blurted out blubberingly. Suddenly all the reporters jumped out of their seats and packed in around the podium. The crush of reporters and cameramen began squabbling and jockeying for position as the Director looked exhausted and disheveled as he pulled out a hanky and began drying his eyes. Davenport and the Director switched places at the podium. Cameras began flashing and cell phones and digital microphones shot up into the air.

"I found out early this morning about Dabney and sold my stock in DPLUS with the intention of buying it back at a rock bottom price. I told Davenport that under no circumstance should Dabney be cleared because I wanted the stock to plummet. While there is ..."

Davenport looked to the back of the room and Anton stood with a couple of uniformed officers. They nodded at each other. He then made his way around the reporters and walked toward the door.

"What do you want us to do sir," asked one of the patrolmen.

"Just wait till he's finished and take him to headquarters and process him," said Davenport and he looked over to Buelfarbel. "You know he's just going to get a slap on the wrist."

"I know, but this was really about C.B. anyway Giles.

Whatever happens to that dipshit's a bonus."

"I agree. Let's go to the Lady and get that drink."

Davenport and Buelfarbel low-fived and walked out of the room.

EPILOGUE

"I'll meet you in there Anton."

"Okay."

Davenport pulled out his phone and called Linda. "Hey Lind ... I know, you told me where you were earlier ... yeah I'm going to be a while, having a few drinks with some new friends ... okay then tell them I said hi ... I'm not sure, a couple hours ... I know I know ... okay see you later ... Bye ... Jesus Linda Bye." Davenport slid the phone in his pocket and shook his head as he walked through the door. He looked around the bar and found McMusker's bulk taking up two or three places at the bar. He must have sniffed Davenport out, because he immediately turned around and made eye contact. McMusker mouthed *Exhausterall* and winked. Davenport mouthed *Fuck you* and smiled. There was a mutual nod between them and Davenport turned and found Kilroy and Buelfarbel sitting at a corner table.

Davenport sat down and they ordered a round of beers. They were both wondering, so Kilroy explained how he faired getting the animals home, which reminded Davenport to give the memory card back to Kilroy, and that started a conversation about the pictures. Buelfarbel brought up the glasses thing with Burgle, and then Davenport went on about the goats and Gamble. Time was flying by as the men laughed and told more stories about the day. Kilroy and his waiting to fill the Ziplock bags had Davenport and Buelfarbel in tears, but every so often a lull in the conversation would arise, and the men sat and gave C.B. his silence, which was always followed by a teary-eyed toast from Kilroy. Though not long after another story would come up and they were laughing again and before they knew it they were deep into eleven o'clock.

"Holy crap it getting late," said Davenport as he checked his phone.

"Yeah I'd better be going too." Buelfarbel pulled out his phone and started texting.

"Kilroy you're not heading out to farm are you," asked Davenport.

"No it's around the corner for me. I'll stay at C.B.'s tonight.

"I really want to thank you guys for today," said Davenport, "I couldn't have done it without you."

"Sure."

"Of course sir. And please I'll take care of the check, it's not often one meets two fine young men in the same day," Kilroy said as he shook both men's hands. "We shall do it again soon I trust."

They both said definitely and see you soon Kilroy.

By the time Davenport walked in the door it was a little after twelve and he threw his keys on the kitchen counter and filled a glass of water and walked to the bedroom.

"Hey."

"Hey Davy did you have a good time," asked Linda as she took her eyes from a book and took off her glasses.

"Yeah it was fun. What a day. I'll tell you all about it tomorrow. Man I'm a little banged up," Davenport said as he rubbed his eyes and sat down on the bed. Linda jumped up on her knees and gave Giles a kiss on his cheek and whispered in his ear. "I have a surprise for you."

"Oh yeah," Davenport said as he took off his shoes.

"Yup. But I have to pee first," Linda said as she hopped off the bed and scampered to the bathroom in her robe. Davenport stood back up, hung up his shirt and pants and climbed into bed. As he turned off the light on his side of the bed Linda walked out of the bathroom.

"Happy anniversary!" she said as the robe fell around her ankles. Black lace teddy, garters, whole nine. Goddamn she's beautiful, thought Davenport. It took him a second but there it was. It wasn't huge but it wasn't fucking small either. Linda smiled and over-cooked a wink as she curtsied.

Davenport shrugged.